CANCELLED

10.1
6 PT

Primary Sources of World Cultures™

IRAN
A PRIMARY SOURCE CULTURAL GUIDE

Lauren Spencer

The Rosen Publishing Group's
PowerPlus Books™
New York

To all the History Teachers I've known

Published in 2004 by The Rosen Publishing Group, Inc.
29 East 21st Street, New York, NY 10010

Library of Congress Cataloging-in-Publication Data

Spencer, Lauren.
Iran: a primary source cultural guide / Lauren Spencer.— 1st ed.
    p. cm. — (Primary sources of world cultures)
Summary: An overview of the history and culture of Iran and its people including the geography, myths, arts, daily life, education, industry, and government, with illustrations from primary source documents.
Includes bibliographical references and index.
ISBN 0-8239-4000-4
1. Iran—Juvenile literature. [1. Iran.] I. Title. II. Series.
DS254.75.S64 2003
955—dc21

2003002202

Manufactured in the United States of America

Cover images: A detail of Arabic script taken from a seventeenth-century Persian illumination *(background)*; the Azadi (Freedom) Tower in Tehran, Iran *(center)*; and an Iranian girl photographed on the streets of Tehran *(right)*.

Photo credits: cover (right), p. 104 © David Turnly/Corbis; cover (center), pp. 40 (bottom), 72, 90, 101 © Alex Fansworth/The Image Works; cover (background), pp. 82, 87 © AKG London; pp. 4 (middle and bottom), 5 (bottom), 12, 15, 17, 21, 23, 30 (top and bottom), 31, 32, 38, 50, 55, 85, 98 (top), 105, 106 © Corbis; pp. 3, 118 © Illustrator map; pp. 4 (top), 13, 91, 93 © Topham/The Image Works; pp. 5 (top), 7, 8, 9, 16, 74 © George Gerster/Photo Researchers; pp. 5 (middle), 96, 98 (bottom), 109, 110 © John C. Stevenson/Peter Arnold, Inc.; pp. 6, 118 (top) © SuperStock; p. 10 © Hideo Haga/The Image Works; pp. 11, 79, 89 © Aurora Photos; pp. 18, 22, 118 (bottom), 45 © The Bridgeman Art Library; pp. 19, 20 © National Museum/Tehran, Iran/The Bridgeman Art Library; pp. 26, 68, 83 © The Granger Collection; pp. 27, 36, 46, 88 © British Library/AKG London; p. 28 © Chehel Sotun/Isfahan, Iran/The Bridgeman Art Library; p. 33 © Olaf Gulbransson/Mary Evans Picture Library; p. 34 © Jerome Delay/AP/Wide World Photos; pp. 37, 99 © Paolo Kock/Photo Researchers; p. 39 © Roger Perrin/The Bridgeman Art Library; p. 40 (top) © Lachenmaier/Bilderberg/Aurora Photos; pp. 42, 78 (top) © Photri-Microstock, Inc.; pp. 43, 48, 76 (bottom) © Art Resource; pp. 51, 64 (top) © Vahid Salemi/AP/Wide World Photos; pp. 52, 53, 56, 58, 59, 69 © Hasan Sarbakhshian/AP/Wide World Photos; p. 60 © Enric Marti/AP/Wide World Photos; pp. 62, 118 (middle) © Diego Lezama Orezzoli/Corbis; p. 63 © Tamashagah-e Pool/Money Museum/Tehran, Iran/The Bridgeman Art Library; p. 64 (bottom) © Roger Wood/Corbis; p. 65 © Koniglichen Bibliothek, Berlin/Mary Evans Picture Library; p. 66 © Mary Evans Picture Library; p. 70 © Helen King/Corbis; p. 71 © Giraudon/The Bridgeman Art Library; p. 73 © Lloyd Cluff/Corbis; p. 75 (top) © Nat and Hanna Brandt/Photo Researchers; p. 75 (bottom) © Reza Abbasi Museum/Tehran, Iran/The Bridgeman Art Library; p. 76 (top) © Michael Nicholson/Corbis; p. 77 © Adam Woolfitt/Woodfin Camp & Associates; p. 78 (bottom) © George Holton/Photo Researchers; p. 84 © AP/Wide World Photos; p. 86 © Francis G. Mayer/Corbis; p. 92 © Cindy Reiman; p. 95 © Reiner Harscher/Aurora Photos; p. 97 © Photo Researchers; pp. 102, 103, 111 © Paul Almasy/Corbis; p. 108 © Shepard Sherbell/Corbis; p. 119 © Illustrator pie chart; p. 120 © Ian Comming/Axiom; p. 121 © Craig Lovell/Corbis.

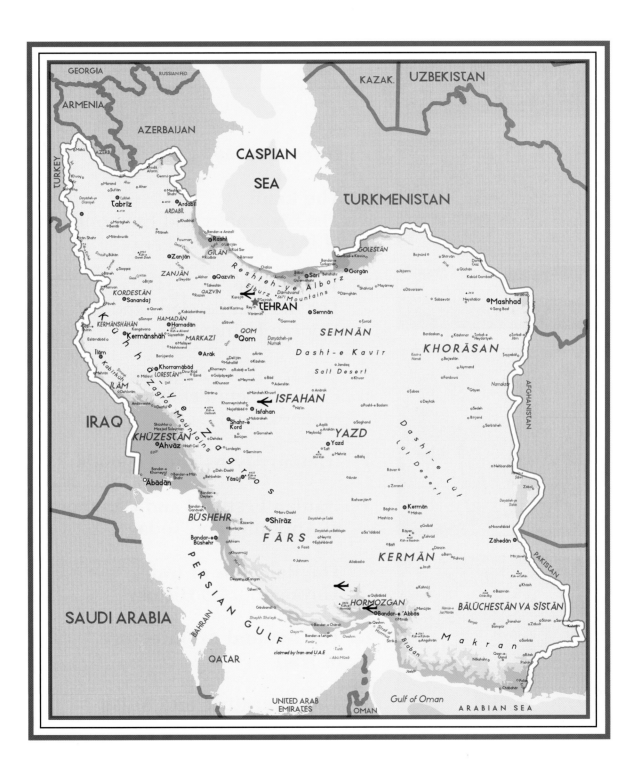

CONTENTS

INTRODUCTION

T he nation of Iran, known as Persia until the early twentieth century, is a land rich in history and culture. Dating back to biblical times, this region holds evidence of some of the world's oldest civilizations. Persia was ruled by kings during its founding centuries, and an Arab invasion in the seventh century brought the teachings of the prophet Muhammad and the religion of Islam into Persia. Thereafter, the majority of Persians became Muslims, as the followers of the Islamic religion are known. They chose to follow the Shiite division, or sect, of Islam, rather than Sunni, which is the sect

that most Muslims follow. In the twentieth century, the reigning *shahs* (kings) brought Iran into a period of modernization, but there were upheavals and disagreements among the more traditional clerics of the country who felt that the nation was becoming too secular (nonreligious). These clerics believed that Iran was too influenced by Western ideas. These opinions, combined with an increasingly restrictive administration, led to the Islamic Revolution of 1979. Afterward, the country became a strict religious state known as the Islamic Republic of Iran and was led by a supreme religious leader known as an *ayatollah*.

Iran is a land of extremes, with vast and treacherous deserts and lush, imposing mountains. It is also a nation rich in natural resources, such as petroleum, which is Iran's number one export. Because of its location at the crossroads of many Middle

The Kermanshah plain *(above)*, in western Iran, is one of the most water-rich areas in the country and the source of the Sepid, Iran's longest river. Rich pastures in this section of the country support large herds of livestock. Tehran *(left)*, the capital city of Iran, is a major industrial center situated at the foot of the Alborz Mountains. With production that largely focuses on food, textiles, cement, and bricks, Tehran is considered a young city, dating back only seven centuries. It has a population of 6.5 million and is the second most populous city in the Middle East after Cairo, Egypt.

This aerial photograph shows the city of Tabriz, the capital of the Azarbaijan province and home to more than one million people. Tabriz is a major tourist destination for both its ancient ruins and its natural mineral springs. Its strategic location in northwestern Iran—surrounded by Iraq to the west, Turkey to the northwest, and Azerbaijan to the north—gives the city both economic and political importance. Besides being the manufacturing, commercial, and transportation center of Iran, Tabriz has, over many centuries, been severely damaged by invasion and natural disasters such as earthquakes. Present-day Tabriz has been built and rebuilt on the ancient site of Tauris, the capital of Armenia during the third century.

Eastern empires, Iran was a major trade link between Europe, Asia Minor, India, and Arabia as far back as the second century BC. Its desert caravans filled with exotic goods traveled along the Silk Road, so-called because of the luxurious Eastern fabrics that made their way west along its path. The exposure and homogenization of many of these Indian and Asian influences created an exotic culture for Iran that is continually expressed in its art, poetry, and cuisine.

From the nomadic sheepherders and villagers who hand-weave beautiful carpets to modern citizens working in major cities like Tehran, Iranians live a life rich in tradition. Although there is no separation between religion and government for most Iranians, its people continue to find ways of exhibiting a distinct individuality, often with a struggle. Since 1979, women have worked to assert themselves with a degree of success. Although they must cover themselves with the traditional veil and robe, they are also the most educated Muslim women in

The thriving city of Minab in southern Iran has mountainous areas as well as plains. Dense vegetation on the outskirts of Minab includes date palm plantations, mango orchards, and farms, which are irrigated by the Minab River.

the Middle East. Vast differences like these are indicative of a country finding its way in a changing global environment. Technology such as the Internet has brought new and different ideas into a nation that has, since the Islamic Revolution, struggled to keep its traditions strong, which has often meant that it also keeps policies of isolation.

Since the hostage crisis of 1979, when sixty-six Americans at the United States Embassy in Tehran were held captive for more than a year, relations between the two countries have been strained. In the 1980s, a prolonged war with neighboring Iraq caused great human casualties and destroyed Iran's economy after the loss of many of its oil wells. But Iran continues to find its own individuality, even as it becomes increasingly modernized. Although the nation's current president, Mohammad Khatami, explores movements to bring the country into the twenty-first century, the Ayatollah Seyed Ali Khamenei—who prefers a more traditional, conservative administration—remains its most powerful leader.

With roughly 70 percent of its current population under the age of thirty, Iran is in a unique position to face the challenge of merging its traditions with modernity in ways that will keep the country vital.

THE LAND

The Geography and Environment of Iran

I ran, a country located in southwest Asia, lies at the heart of the Middle East. It is the sixteenth largest country in the world, just slightly larger than the state of Alaska. With its rugged terrain, Iran is a land of extremes, largely covered with steep mountain ranges and vast deserts. It is bordered in the north by Armenia, Azerbaijan, the Caspian Sea, and Turkmenistan, and in the east by Afghanistan and Pakistan. Turkey and Iraq form Iran's western border, while the country embraces coastal waters in the south in areas bordered by the Gulf of Oman and the Persian Gulf. Iran's territory spans more than 636,292 square miles (1,648,000 square kilometers).

There are three very distinct types of terrain in Iran—mountains, lowlands, and deserts. In the center of the country are high plains and desert plateaus surrounded by a ring of mountain ranges. Coastal lowlands form the bottom of mountains that lead to the sea in the north and the ocean in the south.

The magnificent ruins of Persepolis *(left)*, the capital city of ancient Persia, lie at the foot of Kuh-i-Rahmat, or "Mountain of Mercy." The exact date of Persepolis's founding is not known, but it is assumed that Darius I began construction in the ancient city between 518 and 516 BC. Persepolis was the seat of the flourishing Achaemenid Empire. An Iranian man *(above)* harvests dates. The date palm is the oldest food-producing tree in the world. In Iran, there are 180,000 hectares dedicated to date groves, making the nation the largest producer of dates in the world.

This aerial photograph of the Iranian desert shows one of its major earthquake zones. Iran is located in an active tectonic region with the Arabian plate lying to its south and the Eurasian plate lying to its north. With Arabia slowly pushing northward into Eurasia, Iran rests in its collision zone. Nearly all of Iran is regarded as a high-risk earthquake zone, with several hundred tremors and at least a dozen strong quakes registered there each year. There have been approximately 1,000 recorded earthquakes in Iran over the past two decades.

The Desert Plateaus

Iran's central desert plateau is one of the driest regions on Earth. Its altitude can reach as high as 4,000 feet (1,219 meters) above sea level. On the western side of the Dasht-e Kavir, which is a great salt desert, there are streams and springs that provide permanent water sources. In the past these were often the locations of fertile oases. Today they are home to some of the nation's most active cities, such as its capital, Tehran, the once ancient city of Isfahan, and Qom, a center for many Shiite clerics.

For the most part, the plateaus of Iran's central desert plains are barren landmasses. During ancient times, these deserts were often busy with caravans crossing from China, India, Arabia, Asia Minor, and the Mediterranean. Because Iran, known then as Persia, straddled Europe and Asia, it was an ideal trade route for merchants.

The Sahand Mountains, called the "Bride of the Mountains" by most Iranians, have approximately seventeen peaks reaching more than 9,843 feet (3,000 meters) in height. Located near the city of Tabriz, the area has a variety of flora and fauna. Popular during the winter months, skiing is a major source of income in this region.

One of the desert routes that runs through the Dasht-e Kavir was known in ancient times as the Silk Road. Because it is not made up of sand or gravel, but instead of salty soil, the surface of the desert along this route is especially dangerous. It sometimes forms into a crust after intense heat from the sun dries swampy winter floodwaters. The salty crystal surface of the Dasht-e Kavir is not only painful to walk on, but there is sometimes danger that the crust will break through and pull everything above it into the quicksand below. Ancient tales tell stories of entire caravans traveling over the Silk Road that completely disappeared. In southeast Iran, the Dasht-e Lut, a sand and stone desert, is bare of any vegetation and covered with windswept dunes.

The Mountains

Mountain ranges surrounding Iran in the north and west provide a dramatic backdrop to its desert climate. In northern Iran, the Elburz Mountains rise to the nation's highest peak, known as Mount Damavand, which is 18,605 feet (5,671 meters) high. Damavand is actually a volcanic peak, though there has never been any record of its eruption. The snowy Elburz Mountains rise above the city of Tehran. There are active volcanic peaks in the Elburz that, like the Sahand and Ararat, sputter and spew every few years. This volcanic activity has been linked to earthquakes that periodically shake sections of Iran. In June 2002, a powerful earthquake was responsible for killing at least five hundred and injuring more than a thousand people in the area.

The rugged Zagros Mountains comprise the largest and longest range in Iran. They circle the western portion of the country for 875 miles (1,408 kilometers) beginning from its northwestern corner and moving along its southern border down to the

Qanat

A *qanat* is an underground irrigation tunnel that brings water to cities, villages, and farmlands. Since water is vital and scarce in Iran, early dwellers developed an ingenious system of moving spring, stream, and melting snow water from place to place. Qanats can be more than 50 miles (80 kilometers) long, and are usually about 100 feet (30 meters) below the surface of the land, although some reach depths three times deeper.

The qanat system was developed many centuries ago, with some in operation for thousands of years. They are maintained by workers descending by rope into deep holes in the earth who keep the water's flow moving. Often the job of qanat maintenance is passed down through the generations from father to son.

Persian Gulf. There are streams that flow through the narrow gorges of the Zagros, which are called *tangs*. In the center of the range are many deep and fertile valleys. Because of the difficulty posed in traveling through the Zagros, the people who inhabit the area are largely secluded, often living an extremely isolated lifestyle.

To the east of Iran are the less impressive Khorasan Mountains. Though smaller in size than the Zagros, they shelter lush fertile valleys ideal for sustaining livestock.

Waterways

The source of Iran's only navigable river, the Karun, begins in the Zagros Mountains. A section of it empties into the Persian Gulf, and another tributary forms part of the border between Iran and Iraq. While it might be natural for major bodies of water like the land-locked Caspian Sea in the north, the Persian Gulf in the south, and Lake Urmia in the northwest to drain into the basins of smaller rivers, these waterways instead drain into Iran's deserts. This water then forms saltwater lakes called *namaks* and *kavirs*. The namaks are shallow salt lakes. The kavirs are dangerous because they

The Makran coastal plain, taking its name from the old province of Makran in southeastern Iran, lies along the Gulf of Oman. Its coastline stretches 249 miles (400 kilometers) and is shared by neighboring Pakistan. Just off the Makran Coast, the Arabian Sea is abundant with fish and shrimp, creating a lively fishing industry in this region. The name "Makran," in fact, comes from the Farsi words *mahi khoran* meaning "fish eaters."

are deeper and sometimes form sediment that is muddy and sticky.

Coastal Lowlands

The Caspian shoreline in northern Iran was once the location of Persian trading ports. The ancient Greeks and Persians called the area Hyrcania. Today, there is very little trading across the sea. This area is now densely populated with fishermen who depend on coastal waters for their livelihood. In the south is the coastal lowland of Khuzistan situated at the head of the Persian Gulf. The Shatt-al-Arab waterway makes up the southern stretch of the Iran-Iraq border and is where the Tigris and Euphrates Rivers converge into the Persian Gulf. Many of the world's earliest civilizations existed there, including the Elamite kingdom. Following the coastline east along the Persian Gulf, the mountains and cliffs occasionally retreat from the water, creating narrow coastal plains. One southern coastal plain, called the Makran, is a hot, arid stretch that extends toward Pakistan. For thousands of years, it has been inhabited by villagers whose culture is closely aligned with neighboring Pakistan and India, rather than to Iran. Its residents fish in the Gulf of Oman and cultivate date palms along the areas few streams.

Climate

The climate of Iran is largely dry because of the lack of moisture in the air. Because the country's mountains block incoming ocean breezes, most of the desert land remains incredibly arid. Iran's many waterways also tend to evaporate from this strong heat during the summer months. Only Lake Urmia, in the northwest, is large enough to remain permanent. Since it is a saltwater lake, however, it

The desert dunes seen in this photograph are encroaching upon a small Iranian village. Iran's two great deserts are the Dasht-e Kavir and the Dasht-e Lut.

is not fit for either drinking or irrigating farmland.

There is little rainfall in Iran, with most of it occurring during the winter months of November through April. The southern coast along the Persian Gulf is very humid, while the land stretching into the mountains becomes somewhat lush until it reaches the desert.

During the summer, Iran is divided into two climate zones based on its overall altitude. The *sardsir*, or cool land, classifies all areas that are above 6,500 feet (1,981 meters). Days in this zone are pleasant and breezy followed by cooler evenings. The *garmsir*, or warm land, encompasses all zones at lower elevations from the coasts to the cities. Many Iranians migrate to sardsir regions during the summer months to escape otherwise brutal heat. The coldest region of Iran is in the northwest, across the border from Azerbaijan. In the winter, temperatures in this area can drop as low as -35° degrees Fahrenheit (-37° Celsius). Khuzistan, in the southwest, is the hottest region, with summer temperatures soaring to 131° Fahrenheit (55° Celsius). The city of Tehran is in one of the more moderate climate zones, with temperatures ranging from 27° to 45° Fahrenheit (-2° to 45° Celsius) in January and 72° to 99° Fahrenheit (22° to 37° Celsius) in July.

Iran is famous for its winds. On the Persian Gulf coast, heavy humidity is caused by warm, damp winds that blow across the Arabian Desert. In the north, Iran's freezing temperatures are carried on winds that blow south from Siberia. The *shamal* is a regular wind pattern that is felt from February to October along the Iran-Iraq border. A summer wind, sometimes called "the 120-day wind" because it can howl nonstop from May to August, blows in a westward direction from Pakistan, scorching plateaus with gusts up to 70 miles per hour (112 kilometers per hour).

This photograph shows the Bid Boland Gas Treatment Center in Iran. Petroleum has been the main industry in the country since the 1920s. Iran's other major resources are coal, copper, iron ore, lead, and zinc. Pollution from vehicle emissions, refinery operations, and industrial waste is an increasing problem in Iran.

Natural Resources

Petroleum is Iran's most valuable resource. It accounts for 80 percent of the nation's exports. In ancient times, when escaping gas from natural oil flows deep in the earth was set on fire by lightning, it amazed the Persians so much that they began to worship fire. The country is also rich in minerals such as copper, which is mined at Isfahan, Tarum, and Hamadan. Iron, gold, tin, asbestos, and aluminum are also plentiful.

Sturgeon eggs, or caviar, also come from Iran and originate from the Caspian Sea. Caviar is one of its richest natural resources, as well as a great source of export revenue. Unfortunately, recent pollution has substantially reduced Iran's sturgeon population. Pistachio, also a popular export, grow extremely well in the nation's only naturally irrigated agricultural forests around the Caspian Sea.

More than 10,000 plant species thrive in Iran. They range from the spiny succulents that grow in its deserts, to the evergreens that pepper the mountainous regions. Everything from licorice to henna to saffron can be found on the landscape of Iran. The rose, which is the most popular flower in the country, grows wild, as do orchids, irises, and buttercups. Since 1962, all the forests and pastures have belonged to the government.

Despite its harsh climate, Iran supports a variety of mammals. Mountain lions live in the Zagros Mountains, although a large percentage of the species was eliminated during regular Persian hunting seasons. Tigers make their homes in the forests around the Caspian Sea, but as Iran's lands are being excavated, they are also in danger of extinction. Panthers roam many remote locations, while the population of cheetahs and leopards is waning. Other indigenous animals include antelopes, pigs, and goats.

THE PEOPLE

2

The Ancient Persians and the Modern Iranians

The majority of Iranians are descendants of the country's original settlers. While Iran is a multiethnic society consisting of Azerbaijanis, Kurds, Arabs, Turkomans, Baluchis, Jews, Qashqa'i, and a few Westerners, roughly 51 percent of its citizens are the Aryans and Persians who migrated from central Asia 3,000 years ago.

The name "Iran" comes from the Persian word "Aryanam," meaning "the land of the Aryans." These Aryan nomads came from the areas now known as Europe, central Asia, northern India, Afghanistan, and Russia 1,500 years before the birth of Jesus Christ. They settled in two distinct sections of the region. The Medes settled in the north and east and built a capital called Ecbatana (Hamadan). The southern part of the region, now called Fars, was once known as Parsa (or Pars). As its power spread by way of Cyrus the Great in 533 BC, Persia became the name of the land now known as Iran.

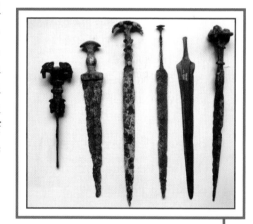

Early History

Archaeologists have sufficient evidence that people were living in the region now known as Iran as far back as 100000 BC. While little is

Six bronze and iron swords (*above*) date back to the Elamite civilization (4000 to 650 BC). The Elamites developed under the influence of nearby Sumerian and Mesopotamian settlements in the Tigris-Euphrates valley. This is an aerial view (*left*) of Takht-e Soleyman, or Solomon's throne, which is located in northwestern Iran. During the early Sassanid dynasty, the entire plateau was fortified with a massive wall and thirty-eight towers. Later, extensive temples were constructed to accommodate the large number of pilgrims to the site.

This wind instrument in the form of a robed woman was created by Elamites between 4000 and 650 BC. The Elamites were a people living in the Zagros Mountains of Persia. The earliest representations of similar instruments were found on relief sculptures of the period, which portray reed pipes, harps, and tambourines.

known about this period of prehistory, about 10,000 years later, Iran was one of the first parts of the world to cultivate a civilization. Settlements at this time supported farming, the domestication of livestock, pottery making, metalworking, and, ultimately, writing. By 6000 BC, a fairly stable culture thrived on the Iranian plateau and in the southwestern area of the country known as Khuzistan. This was the location of some of the world's earliest cities and became known as the kingdom of Elam.

In 3000 BC, there was in place a system of hereditary kingship and an organized priesthood. These people, known as Elamites, gradually spread across the Zagros Mountains and built the city of Susa in the southwest. As this kingdom was growing, waves of Aryans were entering the region from the north, while the Medes were settling in the west and the Persians in the south. The Elamite kingdom flourished until 600 BC when it was conquered by Assyrians from present-day Syria and northern Iraq.

The Achaemenid Empire

The first Persian Empire came into existence around 533 BC when the Persians, known as skillful archers, were led by Cyrus the Great in an overthrow of the Medes. Cyrus became master of the region and named his dynasty the Achaemenid Empire. Within a decade, he went on to lead his troops to conquer the Assyrians, and from then on all the people living in the Iranian region became known as Persians. Cyrus's vast empire included Babylonia, Palestine, Syria, and Asia Minor. Cyrus is most often remembered as a humane leader who allowed his conquered subjects to worship their own religions. In the Bible, he is referred to as the liberator of the Jews, who were held captive in Babylon. He also adopted many artistic and cultural styles of those lands he conquered,

The tomb of Cyrus the Great (d. 529 BC), pictured here, was discovered in 1951 within the ruins of Pasargadae. Known as the Camp of the Persians, Pasargadae was the capital of Persia during Cyrus's reign from 546–529 BC. More than 2,500 years old, the tomb is made of white limestone and stands approximately thirty-six feet (eleven meters) high. The small double-door entrance leads to a windowless room that once contained Cyrus's sarcophagus. An inscription on the tomb, written by Cyrus, reads: "O man, whoever you are and wherever you come from, for I know that you will come—I am Cyrus, son of Cambyses, who founded the Empire of the Persians and was king of the East. Do not grudge me this spot of earth which covers my body."

including the exquisite design of Persian architecture and its artistic motifs. During this time, the Persians built beautiful temples and established trade routes such as the Silk Road in order to make travel safer and easier.

When Cyrus died in 529 BC, he was succeeded by Darius I and then Xerxes, a king who also expanded Persian territory. The Achaemenid Empire then became the largest of its time. Despite the skills of the Persian warriors, the empire was ultimately unable to defend itself against the Greeks.

In 334 BC, Alexander the Great, who was only twenty years of age, swept into Persia and installed himself as its ruler. By 333 BC he had defeated Darius III at the Battle of Issus in present-day Turkey, a conflict that ultimately defeated the Persian forces.

Alexander admired the Persians and even married a Persian princess named Roxana. When he died at thirty-two years of age without heirs, his generals fought among themselves to take control of his territory. General Seleucus finally won its greatest portion, eventually establishing the Seleucid dynasty. His goal was to reestablish Alexander's empire, even campaigning farther eastward into India. Although Seleucus was not nearly as popular as Alexander, he ruled for more than

After the death of Cyrus the Great in 529 BC, his successor, Darius I (d. 486 BC), moved the capital of Persia and called it Persepolis, the ruins of which are shown in this aerial photograph. Persepolis, a name meaning "City of the Persians," was the wealthy seat of government for the Achaemenid kings and a center for receptions and ceremonial festivities. Persepolis was destroyed by Alexander the Great in 330 BC. According to the Greek writer Plutarch, Alexander demolished the palace, setting it on fire, and carried away its treasures on 20,000 mules and 5,000 camels.

forty tumultuous years, many of them spent attempting to restore order to the region.

In the meantime, a group of people called the Parthians established a hold in Persia, living in the center of its desert plateau. While this area was infertile, it did include a long stretch of the Silk Road over which many caravans traveled to and from Asia, Africa, and Asia Minor. The Parthians forced these travelers to pay high tolls and went on to conquer the region, ruling for the next 500 years.

In 224 BC, a Persian named Ardashir I defeated the Parthians, and Persia was returned to Persian rule. Ardashir founded the Sassanid dynasty, which advanced the creation of cities and founded a central governing force. He is also credited with the development of Persian infrastructure such as joined canals and bridges. The following 400 years of Sassanid rule were some of the region's most peaceful. It was also an

economically and culturally rich period. Persian art and literature thrived, and the Persians officially embraced Zoroastrianism, founded by the Persian prophet Zoroaster and considered by some scholars to be the first monotheistic religion. Zoroastrianism had a wide-ranging influence on other world religions that developed in its wake, namely Judaism and Christianity, as it spread throughout the Achaemenid Empire. The first examples of a class system were also developed during the Sassanid dynasty, with priests, warriors, scribes, and commoners all carving out individual places in society.

This stone relief found at Naqsh-i Rustam, an archaeological site in southern Iran, depicts Ardashir I, also known as Artaxerxes (d. 240 BC), receiving his crown from the Persian sun god, Ahura Mazda, on the right. This scene established the religious legitimacy of the Sassanid monarchy, since the duty of Zoroastrianism was to fight evil, allowing the saving redeemer to enter the world.

Although the Sassanids were constantly involved in border wars with the Romans, they did manage to regain the original territories of the Achaemenid Empire. By AD 602, they had attacked the Byzantine Empire, the eastern half of the old Roman Empire, which continued to rule the eastern Mediterranean for centuries after the fall of Rome in 476. The Sassanid dynasty was finally put down by an Arab-led invasion from across the Persian Gulf.

Outside Turmoil

In the early 600s, an Arab named Muhammad who lived in the city of Mecca had a number of religious revelations. He and his followers shaped these into Islam, a new religion that in Arabic means "submission to the will of Allah."

Islam had much in common with Judaism and Christianity, such as its belief in a single god and its shared prophets. After Muhammad's death in 632, Muslims began expanding and conquering surrounding areas. The Islamic Empire began spreading into Asia and Europe.

When Arab warriors defeated the Sassanid Empire in AD 637, they allowed Persians to worship religions other than Islam if they paid the Arabs a tax to do so. Many of the Persian princes and leaders later adopted the Shiite form of Islam, even though Sunni Islam was, and still is, its most common sect. While very few Arabs actually settled in the area that is now Iran, the art and customs of Arabia merged with Persian culture. Soon Arabic became the language of the Persians. The Arabs remained in power for almost 600 years.

Mongol Domination

Early in the thirteenth century, the greatly feared warrior Genghis Khan led Mongol hordes into Persia and brought an end to the Islamic Empire. Cities were destroyed and entire populations of Persians were killed as Khan's grandson Hülegü founded the Ilkhanate dynasty in 1258. The Mongol Empire included territories in modern Iran, Iraq, and parts of Turkey. By 1335, the empire had been fully dismantled, allowing for the short-lived leadership of other more minor dynasties. Descendants of Hülegü broke away from Mongol rule and embraced Islam. Future leaders would also follow Islam, though Timur (also known as Tamerlane or Timur the Lame after he was wounded in his right leg during battle) helped popularize a more mystical sect of the religion known as Sufism.

Timur was a military mastermind who attempted to reestablish Mongol power and its domains. By 1383, he had begun his campaigns into Persia beginning in Herat,

This sixteenth-century Persian miniature painting shows Alexander the Great (356–323 BC) in battle against the Persians. In 331 BC, the Macedonian leader marched to Persia to defeat Darius III and the Persian army, said to number a million men, at the plains of Gaugamela. The Macedonians spotted lights from Persian campfires and encouraged Alexander to lead the attack that night. He refused. Alexander wanted to instead defeat Darius in an equal battle so the Persians would never again raise an army against the Macedonians. The following day, both armies met on the battlefield and Darius fled. Therefore, Alexander was proclaimed king of Persia. When he set out to find Darius , he found the Persian leader dead in his coach, assassinated by his own army for fleeing. Alexander had the assassin executed and gave Darius a royal funeral.

now a city in modern Afghanistan. Timur continued to push his ruthless armies for nearly forty years—heading east into India and north into Russia where his capital was located in present-day Uzbekistan—killing thousands before his own death in 1405.

Timur was succeeded by his son Shah Rukh in 1409, though the empire would never again be as widespread. Maintaining a new capital in Herat, Shah Rukh instead left a legacy as a patron of the arts, supporting a court of miniature painters, including Behzad, and a string of well-versed poets. Ulugh Beg took the throne after Shah Rukh's death in 1447, followed by Uzun Hasan in 1452, after a short period of anarchy in the region. Hasan's territories spanned present-day Iraq, Azerbaijan, and western Iran.

The Safavid Dynasty

In 1501, Persians were once again in power after a family called the Safavids imposed their rule in the region. They were strict Shiite Muslims—in direct opposition with other more liberal interpretations of Islam like Sufism. The most famous of their rulers was Shah Abbas I, who was in power from 1587 to 1629. With the help of an English adventurer named Robert Sherley, Abbas fortified the Safavid army and stopped many invasions of outside tribes, including the Ottoman Turks. His control of the region allowed it to prosper artistically.

Shah Abbas is most often remembered for Persia's times of peace and prosperity because he helped elevate its arts and culture to greater heights. Abbas rebuilt the city of Isfahan, which became the capital of his empire. Isfahan developed into a highly respected Islamic city and was

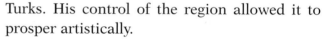

This fourteenth-century Indian miniature painting depicts Timur (1336–1405), also known as Timur the Lame or Tamerlane. Timur, who claimed to be a descendant of Genghis Khan, had a reputation as a cruel conqueror. After capturing cities, he largely slaughtered their inhabitants and built pyramids of their skulls. However, he encouraged art (many times saving artists from his deadly wrath), literature, science, and public works, as well as spread Sufism. Sufism is a mystical sect of Islam whose worshipers gain a connection to Allah through trance and communal dancing ceremonies.

This sixteenth-century miniature painting appeared with the epic poem *Timurnameh* by Persian poet Abdullah Hatifi. It depicts the horrific atrocities committed by Timur and his Mongolian army when they captured Isfahan in 1388. The scene shows looting and murder throughout the city as well as molten metal being poured down the throat of a Persian.

once the intellectual meeting place of artists, the trading center for merchants, and a prized destination of European travelers. Today, many of the original historic monuments, mosques, and bridges built during Abbas's reign remain, symbolic of a time when the city was aptly recalled by sixteenth-century travelers with the phrase "Isfahan is half of the world."

Although Afghans invaded Persia and captured Isfahan, their rule was brief. A Turk named Nader Shah who ruled from 1736 to 1747, protected the city and ousted the Afghan aggressors. He went on to invade Afghanistan and north India and captured the Peacock Throne and the Koh-i-Noor diamond. He then brought these treasures back to Persia to increase the wealth of his empire. As his rule progressed, he grew increasingly paranoid, becoming more tyrannical until he was assassinated in 1747. At the time, civil infighting between various tribes such as the Qajars and the Zands had sparked new violence in the region.

The Qajars

During the nineteenth century, Persia entered a period of turmoil. Although the Qajars took power, establishing the Qajar dynasty in 1794, they ruled for little more than a century. During this time, Persia was mired in political quarrels with Great Britain because of Britain's imperialist policies and Persia's proximity to its newest colonial jewel, India. Great Britain, while protecting the region surrounding India, was involved in a war with Russia, a nation that also wanted power in the region. The recent discovery of oil in Persia, as well as its access to the warm coastal waters of the Caspian Sea, made dominating that region worthwhile for both Russia and Great Britain. Because the Qajar rulers needed financial support, they agreed to certain conditions with both countries in order to obtain loans. Unfortunately, this

Shah Abbas I, known as Abbas the Great (1557–1629), is depicted in this fresco with a courtesan. Abbas was a patron of the arts and sciences. Some of the greatest Persian scholars and scientists lived under his rule, such as Molla Sadra, Mir Damad, Moghaddas Ardebili, and Sheikh Baha-e-Din Ameli. Shah Abbas was responsible for establishing Farsi as the national language of Persia, improving the country's infrastructure, and building some of Isfahan's greatest works of architecture, including the Royal Mosque, the Bridge of Thirty-three Arches, and the famous aqueduct that delivered warm water for public bathing and irrigated elegant gardens.

gave the two superpowers greater control over Persian affairs. At this same time, many Persians became increasingly influenced by Western ideologies, especially after traveling overseas. When these people returned to Persia, they did so harboring ideas of positive change and development. These ideas would soon revolutionize Persia, beginning with the development of its first constitution.

In 1906, Muzaffar al-Din Shah wrote Persia's first constitution establishing a parliament, or *majlis*. This was meant to impose a sense of order in the government and stave off the impending control of the Russians and British, who were busy dividing Persia to suit their own needs. Together, Russian and British leaders divided Persia into three sections, or zones. Russia and Great Britain now controlled two-thirds of Persia with one-third remaining neutral. This division and outside influence, as well as the succession of Mohammed Ali Shah in 1907, reduced the power of the 1906 constitution. Persia was in so much debt to both countries that it remained agreeable.

During World War I (1914–1917), both Russian and British troops were stationed at various times in Persia, and the nation was used as a battleground to reach opposing war zones. Finally, in 1917, the Iran-Soviet Treaty of Friendship was enacted and Russia withdrew from the region. By 1921, a British-supported military officer named Reza Khan seized power in Tehran after a coup, and eliminated the Qajar administration by 1925. Within a year, Reza Khan had crowned himself shah of the new Pahlavi dynasty and had effected a dictatorship.

The Pahlavi Dynasty

In 1935, Persia officially became known as Iran during a period of industrial modernization. The reforms made to the country around this time were immense. They included the establishment of an improved infrastructure, the introduction of civil law codes, a system of banking, and more permanent settlements by nomadic tribes.

Reza Shah made other reforms, too, such as softening religious laws enough to allow women to dress without traditional veils. He also developed international relationships with European countries.

World War II (1939–1945) brought about more upheaval in Iran. Once again, it was the country's geographic location—a strategic link between Europe and Asia—that caused its trouble. Reza Shah favored Germany partly because he resented British and Soviet intrusions of the past, but those same Allied forces still wanted access to Iran's plentiful oil resources. Eventually, it was these same natural resources that led the British and Soviets to invade Iran in 1941. Both nations sent troops into the country to prevent Nazi Germany from gaining control there, easily defeating the Iranian army. Mounting pressure on Reza Shah finally forced him to give up his throne in 1941. He left his throne to his son, Mohammed Reza Pahlavi, who was the last shah of Iran.

Finally, in 1946, the Soviets and British left the region. The postwar years in Iran were a time of economic growth and social change. Although the shah fled the country in the early 1950s during an attempted coup, he returned with more power. The shah now had the support of the United States and Great Britain as well as a secret police force, the Savak, that sought out anyone who opposed him.

Reza Shah Pahlavi (1908–1944), also known as Reza Khan or Reza Shah the Great, is pictured *(center)* in this 1925 photograph with a group of officers. Pahlavi introduced many reforms in Iran such as reorganizing the Iranian government and army. He implemented steps to industrialize Iran by creating a better system of roadways as well as the Trans-Iranian Railway. Pahlavi also modernized the Iranian education system, helped create the University of Tehran, and sent Iranian students to Europe for education. Under his leadership, the country's name changed from Persia to Iran in 1935.

In the early 1960s, the shah introduced what he called the White Revolution, which changed many aspects of traditional Iranian life. Although these reforms were meant to improve the lives of many Iranians, many of the clerics and religious leaders in the country felt that their traditions and beliefs were being disregarded.

The shah was also becoming more tyrannical. By 1975, Iran became a one-party state when the shah outlawed all political parties except his own National Resurgence Party. Anyone who openly criticized him was jailed. Iranian students studying overseas organized anti-shah groups attacking his politics and lavish lifestyle. Although there was rapid industrial growth in Iran, agricultural growth in the country had drastically dropped. This decline led to a dramatic increase in the country's food imports, now more than one-third of the nation's total consumption. Iran's tribal areas

A Russian crew in Iran inspects a fighter plane called the Douglas A-20 Havoc. When Reza Shah Pahlavi seized power, he abolished all special rights granted to foreign powers in Iran in order to gain increased independence for the country. He sought to establish democracy in Iran while achieving freedom from foreign interference.

were also experiencing unrest, and, in 1979, the shah fled the country for a final time.

Islamic Revolution

Religious leader Ayatollah Ruhollah Khomeini, exiled in France during the shah's reign, had been gaining increased support among Islamic Iranians eager to return the country to a more traditional way of life. These Iranians were angered by the increase of Western influences in Iran, which they considered an insult to Islamic beliefs. Buoyed on the wave of this religious fervor, Khomeini swept into the country. He declared Iran an Islamic republic, putting an end to 2,500 years of monarchy, and established a theocratic republic, or one ruled by religious authority. Women were again ordered to veil themselves, and severe punishments were leveraged against anyone who disregarded Islamic laws. Many people fled the country because of the new restrictions.

During World War II (1939–1945), Russian premier Joseph Vissarionovich Stalin (1879–1953), U.S. president Franklin D. Roosevelt (1882–1945), and British prime minister Winston Churchill (1874–1965) *(shown left to right)* met in Tehran in 1943 to discuss the next strategic step against Germany. At the conference, Stalin agreed to maintain an eastern front against Germany, while the Western Allies attacked through France. The "big three" also discussed the possibility of Russia entering the war against Japan and the future creation of an international organization to maintain world peace.

This cartoon by Olaf Gulbransson appeared in the German magazine *Simplicissimus* on July 13, 1908, and depicts Mohammed Ali Shah overthrowing the Iranian constitution granted just two years earlier. In 1906, due to demands by Iranians to modernize Iran, Muzaffar al-Din Shah proclaimed a constitution that limited royal power and created a legislative parliament.

Before long, Iran's economy disintegrated and its rate of unemployment rose. As more Iranians lost their jobs, the inflation rate in the country increased. Civil disobedience grew more widespread. Most Iranians faced a lifestyle of poverty, while the country itself grew wealthier from its abundant oil reserves. Many minorities who had hoped for increased freedoms once the shah left were disappointed at the rigid restrictions put in place by Khomeini. The dramatic drop in oil production and exportation, a result of the revolution, also caused panic in industrialized countries that depended on Iranian resources.

As a result of the United States's support of the shah and the increased pressure by the West for a more liberal Iran, a group of Iranian students stormed the American Embassy in Tehran on November 4, 1979, taking sixty-six Americans hostage. Iran had sent the United States a clear message: It was voicing its displeasure with Western attitudes. After thirteen hostages were initially released, the fifty-three who remained were not let go until January 1981, 444 days later.

Iranian government officials sit under a huge mural of the late Iranian leader Ayatollah Ruhollah Khomeini (1902–1989) on the twelfth anniversary of his death in 2001. Khomeini did not participate in politics during the 1930s, believing that political activities should only be in the hands of religious scholars. During that time he accepted the decision of Ayatollah Haeri to remain passive toward the reforms of Reza Shah Pahlavi against the traditional culture of Islam. However, by 1955, his outlook changed in response to the increased Westernizing of the country, marking the beginning of his protests for a return to conservative Islamic ideals. By 1979, he had returned to Iran from exile in France and was proclaimed leader of the country's revolution.

The shoppers captured in this 1999 photograph are in a congested *souk*, or marketplace, in downtown Tehran. Today, Iran is a nation of more than sixty-six million people. Now politically stable, Iran is considered a unified nation-state that is aimed at creating favorable relations with neighboring countries. Many Iranians, however, still remain moderately xenophobic, which means that they are fearful of foreigners. Iran's new achievements continue to increase the overall confidence and trust of its citizens.

During the better part of the 1980s, Iran was embroiled in a border dispute with Iraq that sapped its resources. Fighting continued for eight years between the neighboring nations. Further conflicts were launched by Iran's Kurdish population, who used the war to fight for a state of their own, gaining control of a small portion of northern Iraq.

When Ayatollah Khomeini passed away from a heart attack in 1989, Ali Khamenei took over as supreme leader of the country. While the spiritual leader, or *walifaqi* as they are officially called, is considered the supreme voice of Islam, there is also a president who is elected by the people. While he has no control over the military, police, or justice system, the president does have a voice in the government. President Ali Akbar Rafsanjani held the office for two full terms, from 1989 to 1997, when the current president Mohammad Khatami was elected. He is now serving his second and final term.

Modern Iranians

Because the central desert regions of Iran are incredibly harsh, most people live in Tehran, Isfahan, and Shiraz, in the northern and western sections of the country. Some lead a nomadic existence, while others form small clans in the mountains often isolated from the rest of the populace.

Areas in Iran are often called by regional tribal names. For example, Luristan, in the Zagros Mountains, is the home of the Lurs, while Sistan-Baluchistan in the southeast, is the home of the Baluchis along the Pakistan-Iran border. Iran is divided into twenty-eight provinces, called *ostans*, with many of the inhabitants retaining the traditional dress and language of each region's descendants.

Many minority groups, such as the Azeris, the Baluchis, and the Kurds, supported the 1979 revolution because they believed that once the shah was gone they could achieve the independence for which they had fought. But that did not prove true. Khomeini continued to give power only to traditional Iranian government officials. He even abolished democratic representation of minority groups in parliament.

Iran also has a small percentage of nomads. These tribal people spend their lives moving from one area to another, establishing semipermanent homesteads. They live traditional self-sufficient lifestyles where hunting and herding provide them with food, milk, and animal hides for cloth and tents. Women spin yarn and weave cloth, rugs, and other items, which are often bartered for different goods. Although these nomadic tribes are counted in census numbers, they often live independently of government rule, systematic schooling, and state-provided services.

THE IRANIAN LANGUAGE

3

From Ancient Persian to Modern Farsi

F arsi, a modernized form of Persian, is the official language of Iran and one of the world's oldest languages. Its name comes from the ancient word "Pars," which was an area in the southwest of the Persian highlands during the time of the Achaemenid Empire. Later, during the Islamic conquest in the seventh century, Arabic influence brought about a change of that region's name from Pars to Fars and the name of the language became Farsi.

Farsi is an Indo-European language, which means that it is a part of a large group of dialects that includes English, German, and French. Although Farsi was first written in an Arabic script after the Arab invasions, it has absolutely no relation to Turkish or Arabic.

Historians define the Persian-Farsi language in three distinctions: Old Persian, spoken and written by the Achaemenids beginning in the sixth century BC; Middle Persian, spoken by the Sassanids between the third and seventh centuries AD; and New Persian, the language spoken since the ninth century. Until the Arab invasion, Persian was written using an Assyrian alphabet. Examples of this can be seen in ancient Persian rock carvings. After the Islamic conquest, Arabic script became the written form of Persian with the addition of several

This illustration from a seventeenth-century edition of the *Shahnameh*, or the *Book of Kings (left)*, depicts the battle between the Iranians and the Turanians. The *Shahnameh* was originally written by the eleventh-century Persian poet Firdawsi (940–1020) and contains rhymed verses recounting Persia's myths, legends, and history prior to the seventh-century Islamic conquest. This example of Cuneiform writing *(above)* was found at the ruins of Persepolis. Cuneiform utilized wedge-shaped strokes, inscribed mainly on clay, stone, metals, and wax. Persian cuneiform is the simplest and most recent, dating between 550 to 330 BC, and it uses thirty-six characters, mostly alphabetic.

This illuminated manuscript page was taken from a Koran, the Islamic holy book of Allah's laws that were received by the prophet Muhammad. It was once necessary for Persians to possess a working knowledge of Arabic to read the Koran, which was originally written in Arabic. Translations of the Koran are often considered blasphemous, though attempts are being made to translate it into Farsi, the national language of Iran.

characters to accommodate special sounds. This form of Persian-Farsi is written and read from right to left and is still used today.

New Persian has remained virtually unchanged since the eleventh century AD. At that time it was used to write the *Shahnameh* (the *Book of Kings*), a series of 60,000 couplets (two lines of verse that rhyme) narrating the history of Persia and written by a poet named Firdawsi (also spelled Firdusi, Ferdowsi, Firdousi, or Firdausi). The Persian language was the diplomatic tongue for the entire Arab world, since Persia was the dominant conquering empire of the time. It was spoken at the court of the Turkish sultan in Istanbul and also in major cities such as Baghdad, Damascus, and Cairo. As the Persian Empire declined, so did the use of traditional Persian in countries outside of Iran. The modern spoken form of Persian, or Farsi, is very different from the literary form of New Persian.

Modern Farsi

During the time of Reza Shah in the 1930s, a purification of the Persian language was instituted when the shah restored forgotten expressions and vocabulary. This effort, combined with the infusion of added foreign influences that came from increased overseas travel, added new dimensions to the language. Many Iranians returned home speaking English, French, German, and Russian, and until the revolution in 1979, the streets of Iran hummed with a variety of expressions and dialects.

Today, the Iranian government discourages this linguistic diversity, with Arabic being the only exception because it is the language used for the Koran (Qur'an), the holy book of Islam. But with new technology influencing world culture and most of the population literate (85 percent) and young (70 percent are under the age of thirty), English, French, and Russian expressions have found their way into modern Farsi.

Some of the most charming things about Iran and its abundant rules of behavior are the expressions commonly exchanged during regular daily interactions. For instance, greetings spoken in Farsi have typical responses. Like the English response of "You're welcome" after a person expresses thanks, Iranians have numerous standard replies to various situations and expressions. Iranians will almost always apologize for turning their back to someone, to which that person would respond, *"gul pusht-eh ruh nadareh,"* or "a flower has no back." To compliment an Iranian on his or her appearance, the common Farsi expression is, *"cheshm-tan ghashang meebeeneh,"* or "Your eyes see beautifully." After eating a fine meal, an Iranian might respond *"Dast-e shoma dard nakoneh,"* or "May your hands not be tired."

A Variety of Languages

While roughly 58 percent of the population in Iran use Farsi as their language, there are other ethnic groups that have their own specific dialects. The Azeris are one of these prominent and traditional groups. Having settled in the northwest section of Iran since the tenth century, and as direct descendants

This miniature painting was taken from a nineteenth-century manuscript of *One Thousand and One Nights*, also known as the *Arabian Nights*, an internationally popular anthology of tales originally written in Arabic. *One Thousand and One Nights* began as stories told orally and was preserved and transcribed by Arabs in the Middle Ages. Like many myths, there is no single author, and the stories are derived from various Middle Eastern and Asian cultures. Some scholars believe that the framework of the whole collection, in which Queen Shahrazad avoids execution by telling tales for one thousand and one nights, is the same story as that of the biblical Book of Esther.

This carpet dealer sells his wares at a bazaar in Isfahan under signs in various languages including Arabic, Farsi, and Chinese. Farsi, also called Persian, is the official and literary language of modern Iran as well as the country's most widely spoken tongue. Farsi has changed very little in the past eleven centuries, and an educated Iranian can read works written a thousand years ago without difficulty. This language has left an imprint on Turkish and Urdu, the language of Pakistan, which is also spoken in Afghanistan, India, Iraq, and parts of eastern Africa.

of the Turks, they speak Azari, which is a Turkish dialect. Although mainly farmers, herders, and traders who are isolated in their villages, the Azeris are a stable part of Iranian society. Other groups include the Qashqa'i, nomads from the highlands who speak a Turkish dialect, and the southeastern Brahui, whose language and culture comes from their roots in India.

Body Language

Iranians tend to be very expressive with their arm gestures and facial expressions. They can show warmth, frustration, or friendliness with just a movement of their hands or expression of their face. And while some of their common

In Tehran, park signs warn women to wear *chadors*, the large circular cloths that cover the wearers' bodies from head to toe. Although dress codes for Iranian women have softened, there are continued requirements that all Iranians must follow, such as avoiding the exposure of flesh or wearing bright colors. The sole limitation for working women is the restrictive chador, which must not be fastened but instead physically held shut with one hand at all times.

movements may look similar to Western gestures, they mean completely different things in Iran. For instance, the thumbs-up movement we might use to signal "good job" or "well done" is an offensive gesture to Iranians and is not used except to show anger.

While Iranians may show more expression individually, they are much more contained in public during normal interaction. Unlike in Western nations, there are more barriers for Iranians that have to do with gender and societal status. For example, men and women are forbidden to touch each other in public, even if they are married. Young people who have grown up under the rule of the ayatollahs have recently been testing the boundaries of Islamic rules by holding hands or showing public affection, which can lead to severe punishments. Often these outward displays are discouraged or stopped by men who act as guardians of public morals. These men are called *Basij*, a term that originated with the members of a loose-knit Islamic militia.

Persian and Farsi

These well-known English words originated from the Persian language: shawl, pajama, taffeta, khaki, kiosk, divan, lilac, jasmine, julep, jackal, caravan, bazaar, checkmate, and dervish.

From English to Farsi:

Yes	bale
No	na, nakher
Please	lotfan
Thank you	motashakkeram
Excuse me	bebakhshid
Good-bye	khoda Hafez
Good night	Shab bekheyr

President Khatami has brought about a slight loosening of the strict fundamentalism that governs public interactions, but overall, the rigid rules of Iran's Islamic constitution remain lawful, keeping men and women separated from each other in public. Even today, any woman who is seen shaking hands with a man in public could be jailed.

How a woman dresses in public is also regulated. The purpose of *hejab*, the Islamic dress code, is to make women look anonymous by clothing them in the same traditional dark-colored headscarf, veil, and *chador*, or cloak, which is supposed to provide coverage from head to toe.

IRANIAN MYTHS AND LEGENDS

4

Myths of creation, often very different depending on the culture in question, explain how the world came into being through the relationship of nature and humans. In Iran, this creation myth is recorded in a book called the *Bundahishn*, which literally means "the creation." It is also referred to as *Zand-agahih* (Knowledge from the Zand) and tells the story of the earth's origin. It was compiled in the eighth and ninth centuries and was based on Zoroastrian beliefs, which was the religion of the ancient Persians before Islam.

The *Bundahishn*

The *Bundahishn* has three main themes: the creation of the earth, of animals, and of people. According to this myth, the sky was the first part of the world to be created. It looked like a round empty shell made of crystal. Water was created next, followed by the earth. Originally it was believed that the earth was flat, a belief shared by the majority of creation myths. Plants and animals came next, followed by humans, and finally fire. Once all of these elements were in place, life—and its conflicts—began to form.

The Zagros Mountains *(left)* dominate the landscape of western Iran. The ongoing search for the remains of Noah's ark continues there today, though many people believe the ark landed atop Mount Ararat in Turkey. Only recently have scholars theorized that the ark could have landed instead in Iran. From a room located in Persepolis, this stone relief (above) depicts a Persian king in combat with the monster Alato, a symbol of the demon god Ahriman. The face of the Persian king was intentionally damaged and is believed to be that of the hated king Xerxes.

The entire world was formed into seven separate landmasses when the god of rain, known to Iranians as Tistar, brought great floods that covered the universe and divided the earth. The Tree of All Seeds, or Tree of All Remedies, grew out of the ocean and carried all the varieties of plants across the earth. This massive tree was home to the legendary bird named Saena, who had great powers of protection for all living things. Another plant growing nearby the Tree of All Seeds was the Gaokerena, which had healing properties when eaten and was said to revive the dead.

Iran's northernmost mountains, the Elburz, were believed to be the first to grow out of the earth, over the course of eight centuries. According to the *Bundahishn*, these mountains had roots that grew deep into the ground with peaks surrounded by a spinning variety of celestial bodies that included the stars, the moon, and the sun. As the mountains developed from the earth, rivers began to flow down their sides circling the world to the east and west before flowing back up to its peak. It was this return journey that allowed the water to become purified before it began its journey down the mountains again.

The *Bundahishn* also explains the origins of animals such as a white bull or ox named Goshorun. The bull was killed by the evil spirit Angra Mainyu (the word "anger" has its roots in *angra*), who then carried a piece of the animal to the moon. The animal's flesh was then purified, becoming the source of all the animal species on the earth. On the opposite side of the river from where Goshorun had been created lived the first man. His name was Gayomartan, and he was said to be as wide as he was tall and also "as bright as the sun." Angra Mainyu also killed Gayomartan, but he was instead purified by the sun after his death and planted as a seed from which a rhubarb plant grew. From this rhubarb grew Mashya and Mashyanag, the first living man and woman. Just as in the Christian and Jewish stories of Adam and Eve, an evil spirit (again, Angra Mainyu) deceived them and they were removed from the garden of paradise and forced to wander in an evil world. Fifty years would pass before the couple could produce children, a set of twins. But the blessed event was filled with horror when Mashya and Mashyanag ate both infants. Finally, after another long period of childlessness, another set of twins was born. As the story goes, it was from these children that the entire human race developed.

The *Shahnameh*

The Persian *Book of Kings*, known as the *Shahnameh*, was written over a thirty-year period during the tenth century by a Khorasan poet named Firdawsi (AD 940–1020).

This illustration was taken from a fifteenth-century edition of the *Shahnameh*, or *Book of Kings*, originally written in 1010. Firdawsi wrote the epic poem about Persia's history in order to prevent the myths, legends, and heritage of his people from being lost forever. In writing the *Book of Kings*, he also limited the use of Arabic words, which created a new power and pride in the Persian language and served as testimony to the independence and heritage of Persia. The *Book of Kings* stands as the embodiment of the Persian worldview, culture, and history and is regarded as the foremost document about Iran.

It is Iran's best-known work and an epic poem that explains the history of Persia. Spanning more than 4,000 years, it details the history of the empire from its earliest beginnings to its decline and conquest by Arab forces. The *Shahnameh* combines factual history and fictional legends in an astounding series of 60,000 rhyming couplets. Intricately woven, it is an epic story of shahs and the queens and princesses who dazzled them. It revolves around the coming of Rustam, a mythical warrior whose father was raised by a great winged bird. The verses relate magical tales of lands conquered by dragons and superior beings with superhuman powers.

The events are described in a writing style that is both magical and exaggerated but that is symbolic of actual events in Persian history. Everyone in Iran—from the city of Tehran to the mountains of Elburz—knows of this poem and its contents and can easily recite its verses. The *Shahnameh* has also been copied and illustrated by some of Iran's greatest painters and calligraphers. It is just one of Iran's most culturally rich offerings and a testimony to the strength of Persian poetry and storytelling.

The word "fairy" can also be traced to the *Book of Kings*. It was taken from the Persian word *peri*, a mythical figure that appears in many legends. In one legend, a Persian romance called *Hatim Tai*, the peries are magical winged figures that are waged in a war with the evil *deevs*. The peries represent light, while the deevs are symbolic of darkness. Over time, the word "peri" was transformed phonetically into "fairy," which then found its way into current European translations.

The Importance of Dreams

The interpretation of dreams holds great importance in Persian culture. Firdawsi used dream sequences in the *Book of Kings* to enliven the action, to create more detailed characters, and to bring symbolism into his poetry. His opinion was that "enlightened souls see

This sixteenth-century Persian miniature painting, another scene from the historical *Book of Kings*, depicts a bathing scene and is housed in the British Library in London. Firdawsi, the poem's author, is now considered one of the most important Persian poets, but during his lifetime, the Turkish king to whom Firdawsi presented his work rejected it because it did not contain any references to Turks. As a result, Firdawsi died an impoverished and grief-stricken man. An earlier edition of the manuscript is located in Firdawsi's shrine in the Iranian village of Tus and weighs 161 pounds (73 kilograms).

dreams in all existing things." Often throughout the poem, dream sequences include symbols and foreshadow the details and tone of future events. Firdawsi said that it was the act of dreaming that helped him complete the *Book of Kings*, giving him the strength to see the project to the end.

From a Shiite Muslim point of view, dreams may take on a mystical inner meaning that is somewhat aligned with a religious or spiritual enlightenment. Dreams are normally divided into two main categories. There are the dreams that happen during sleep and those that occur in a semiconscious state. This semiconscious dream state is marked by a sense of ecstasy and often includes a mental departure from the body, sometimes guided by an angel or a winged creature. These dreams are then written down and studied by religious figures and prophets. Dreams are crucial to their religious strength. All of the *imams* (spiritual guides) are considered to have had dreams that inspired their devotion to Allah. They are often called upon to interpret the symbolic dreams of others. The imams feel that the dreams of believers are always true and will lead to greater spiritual enlightenment. They also believe that a person must perform certain acts

Jinni

According to the Koran, Allah created a being called a jinni from "smokeless fire" before the creation of man. Angels were created from light, jinni from fire, and man from mud and clay. The word "jinni" originated from the Arabic *janna*, which means to hide or conceal. It is also a source of the English word "genie." Jinnis are invisible beings that can take on the shape of humans or animals. They are said to be mischievous and fiery and are referred to in the Koran as troublemakers or evildoers. If they choose a human form, they can exist alongside mankind and can eat, drink, and function on Earth. Islamic lore often attributes the sightings of alien figures or ghosts to the existence of jinnis, and there are often debates among Muslims about whether Satan comes from the world of jinnis.

in order to become a visionary. Dreams also play an important role in the Shiite tradition of *welaya*, which is the elevation of an imam to be a guardian of Islamic beliefs. All Muslims believe that imams who have been visited in dreams are on the right path to enlightenment.

In the past, women known as *shamans* have always held an important role in Persian society as healers and prophets. They were often seen as an important link between the physical and spiritual world. While the current spiritual leaders of Iran are male, it is important to remember that women have played important roles in Persian history, too.

Queen Esther

Esther (meaning star of happiness in Hebrew, and derived from the Babylonian goddess of love, Ishtar) was a young Jewish woman who lived in Susa, then the capital of Persia, in 599 BC. After her parents died, she lived with her uncle Mardochai. When King Assuerus, ruler at the time, became angered at

Queen Esther begs King Assuerus to intervene on behalf of the Persian Jews in this illustration taken from an eighteenth-century manuscript of the Scroll of Esther, a story commonly read during the Festival of Purim. The tombs of Esther, queen of Persia, and her uncle Mardochai, are located in Hamadan, Iran, and are visited by Jewish pilgrims from all over the world.

his current wife's refusal to attend a royal banquet, he divorced her. He then ordered the most attractive maidens brought to his court so he could choose another. Esther was chosen to be his wife. She was allowed to bring her uncle Mardochai along with her to court as her adviser. One day, Mardochai overheard a plot to kill the king and reported it to Queen Esther, who told King Assuerus. Before long, the offenders' plan was stopped. Mardochai was hailed as a great man for saving the king's life. In the meantime, Aman, a favorite of the king's court, had decided that Mardochai did not show him the proper respect and organized a plan to kill him by slaughtering all the Jews of the kingdom. Mardochai, having learned of this planned massacre, pleaded with Esther to beg the king to intervene and stop the impending bloodshed.

Esther was fearful of entering the royal chamber without being summoned, a crime punishable by death, until she realized that the fate of her people rested squarely upon her shoulders. Soon, she devised a plan. She told the Jews of the city to fast and pray for three consecutive days, at the end of which time she would visit the king and beg for their salvation. On the third day, she approached the king, who received her happily and told her that he would grant any request she desired. She asked that he and Aman dine with her, an evening when she revealed the attack planned upon her people. The king believed her story and ordered Aman to be hanged, while telling the Jewish people of the kingdom that they had the right to defend themselves. Mardochai declared the Feast of Purim as a day of memory in which the Jews were to be killed, but instead, because of Queen Esther's bravery, it became a day of celebration.

The Iranian people also embrace Esther's story, which is told in the Bible and the Torah, the book of wisdom and laws of the Jewish faith. She is buried in the city of Hamadân, where a Torah lies open next to her tomb.

IRANIAN FESTIVALS AND CEREMONIES OF ANTIQUITY AND TODAY

5

Westerners can gain an accurate understanding of the importance of Islam in modern Iran just by the priority its citizens place on the religion's many rituals, festivals, and holidays. These festivities follow the Arab-Islamic lunar calendar, so the dates of each celebration change from year to year. Just as significant are Iran's national secular holidays, which take place during specific dates.

Now Ruz

One of the most spectacular Iranian holidays is Now Ruz (also Nowruz, Norouz, Norooz). It is the celebration of the Iranian New Year and begins on the first day of spring each year (March 21). In Farsi, Now Ruz means "new day," and the holiday is meant to celebrate new life, leaving the darkness of winter behind and entering the light of spring. Though widely considered a national holiday, it

Kurdish villagers *(left)* dance in preparation for a wedding in the village of Ghara Kilissa. Kurdish weddings involve much folk dancing, often with routines that date back hundreds of years. Frequently the main events of a Kurdish wedding, the dances signify the unification of the Kurdish community and recognize the bride and groom as a newly married couple. An Iranian man *(above)* reads the Koran during the holy month of Ramadan. Ramadan is the ninth month of the Muslim lunar calendar and a time of intense worship. Throughout Ramadan, Muslims fast during daylight and eat only a small evening meal after sunset in order to focus their energy on reading the Koran, doing good deeds, giving alms (charity), and purifying their behavior.

An Iranian man dances as he celebrates the festival of Sizdeh Bedar, the last day of the Persian New Year. Sizdeh Bedar, meaning "the thirteenth outdoors," marks the thirteenth day of Now Ruz, which begins on March 21. According to the *Book of Kings*, Now Ruz started several millennia ago during the reign of mythological King Jamshid. Jamshid defeated the demons and brought prosperity to his subjects, becoming master of everything but the heavens. To reach skyward, Jamshid had a throne built entirely of jewels and ordered the demons to lift him to the sky. The Persians were so amazed at his power on that occasion that they showered him with gifts, the anniversary of which is now known as Now Ruz.

actually has its roots in the Zoroastrian religion. Stone carvings dating back to the Achaemenid Empire in the twelfth century BC show kings receiving gifts and entertaining large groups of people during one of the first Now Ruz festivals.

The celebrations traditionally last for thirteen days and involve many important rituals. Shab-e-chahar Shanbeh Suri (The Eve of Red Wednesday) begins the celebration marking the last Wednesday of the solar year. On the Tuesday night before, families gather to give thanks for the past fortune and the opportunity to decrease future misfortune through the cleansing of fire, an important element in the Zoroastrian religion. The family then builds a bonfire and leaps over it while singing *"Sorkhie to az man o zardie man be to!"* a phrase that translates to "Give me your red color, take away my sickly pallor." Fireworks have also become a part of the New Year tradition, although they are against the law in most urban cities.

The act of cleaning is also an important ritual to begin Now Ruz. Families thoroughly clean their homes during this time, often washing curtains or draperies, beating rugs, or buying new furniture and fabrics. It is also considered customary to purchase new clothing during this time of year. Then, on the first day of New Year, Iranians visit with friends and other family members.

Before the holiday, a table is set with seven symbolic items. This ritual is called *haft sin*. "Haft" means "seven." Seven of the items on the table start with the Farsi letter *sin*, which is the English *s*. This display is usually set up a few weeks ahead of the celebration, sort of like how decorations are displayed before Christmas. The items on the table represent truth, justice, good thoughts and deeds, prosperity, virtue, immorality, and generosity. They are *sabzeh* (sprouted seeds), *sib* (an apple), *sonbol* (the hyacinth flower), *sir* (garlic), *senjed* (a dried jujube fruit), *somagh* (lemon pepper), and *sekan* (vinegar). Other offerings on the table are often *shirii* (pastries), lighted candles (fire), a mirror to reflect the candlelight, colored eggs (for fertility), a bitter orange floating in water (the cosmos), coins (prosperity), the Koran or book of poetry, and a bowl with goldfish because they are considered lucky. Iranians spend this holiday at home socializing with family, eating a variety of celebratory dishes including *ash reshteh* (noodle soup), *kookoo sabzi* (herbed omelet), or *sabzi pollo ba mahi* (herbed fish and rice). Together the clan awaits the transition to the new year.

The thirteenth day of New Year—one that is considered unlucky—marks the end of the break for schoolchildren. Families leave their homes for outdoor activities such as picnics. These activities are meant to thwart bad luck and are called Sizdeh Bedar (*sizdeh* means "thirteen" and in English this phrase translates to "getting rid of thirteen"). One of the rituals performed during the picnic is the discarding of the sabzeh, as it has supposedly absorbed all the pain and hardship that may lie in wait for the family during the coming year. Sometimes young women will tie the leaves of the sprouts together before tossing them into a stream as a symbol for wanting to be wed.

Other Iranian holidays also originated with the Persians, including Shab-e Yalda, or Rebirth Night, which occurs every year on the winter solstice, or the longest night of the year. Originally the Persians stayed awake for the entire night, keeping their home fires burning to ward off evil spirits. Nowadays, Iranians often light candles or stay up late reciting poetry. Like the celebration of Halloween in the West, children often take to the streets in search of treats and candy, and though not dressed in costume, they may instead bang pots and pans. Others might celebrate with parties, music, and dancing.

Religious Holidays

While Now Ruz dates back to the days before Islam, religious days of observance are crucial in the lives of Iranians. Each week all business are closed on Fridays since the Koran recognizes that day as the holiest of the week, according to the wishes expressed by Allah to the prophet Muhammad. Muslims spend this day in contemplation and prayer.

Ramadan (or Ramazan) is the most holy month of the Muslim calendar. It marks the time that Muhammad spent in the desert near Mecca receiving the word of Allah, which would later become the Koran. The month of Ramadan is always the ninth month of the Islamic lunar calendar, which is based on the cycle of the moon.

Ramadan is a month to focus on the glories of Islam and the teachings of the Koran. Muslims fast, or go without food or drink, from dawn to dusk during each

day of Ramadan. Muslims cannot perform any activities that might distract them from thoughts of Allah. After sunset, Muslims generally feast, since this is the time in which to eat and drink liberally.

The twenty-first and twenty-second days during the month of Ramadan are observed as days of mourning for Ali ibn Abi Talib, Muhammad's son-in-law. Believers in Shia Islam, a sect of the Islamic faith and basis for the Shiite branch of Islam, share the opinion that caliphs must be direct descendants of the Prophet, such as Ali's sons Hussein (also known as Husayn) and Hassan. Ali is remembered during these two days for his suffering in

Iran's supreme leader, Ayatollah Seyed Ali Khamenei (1939–), leads a prayer ceremony during the Muslim festival of Eid al-Fitr. Eid al-Fitr marks the end of the Muslim holy month of Ramadan. This religious holiday celebrates the goodness that the Muslims have received from Allah. Every household that can afford it must pay a tax in the form of food or money, which is then given to the poor. During the celebrations, children usually receive small amounts of money, sweets, or toys, and families visit friends, go to street fairs, and get together for large traditional feasts.

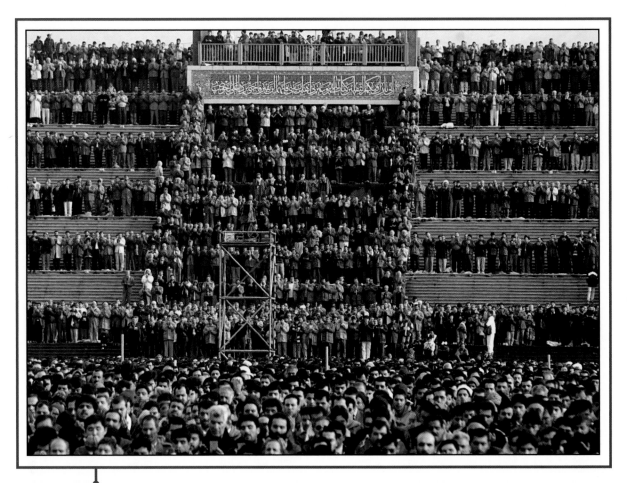

Thousands of Iranians pray at the Imam Khomeini Mosque in Tehran on Eid al-Fitr. On the morning of this important Islamic holiday, Iranians wake early for prayers, which are held in huge mosques or in large open areas, about eighty minutes after sunrise. Special prayers that are reserved only for this day are recited. Also, Iranians exchange greetings of "*Eid-Mubarak*," meaning "a blessed Eid."

the face of nonbelievers. Shiite Muslims beat their breasts and cry to show their religious devotion. Once the new moon rises—as declared only by a religious leader—Ramadan ends.

At this same time, one of the happiest of Muslim festivals begins, the Eid al-Fitr, or the festival of the Breaking of the Fast. At this celebration, Iranian sweets and snacks are placed on decorated tables and everyone eats, laughs, and discusses their hopes for the coming year. Community prayers are held in the mosques, and Iranians invite people into their houses for feasts.

A solemn religious observation in Iran is known as Muharram, which is a month of mourning (also observed on the lunar calendar, so its date changes every year) that marks the martyrdom of Imam Hussein. Because

Holidays and Festivals

Many holidays are based on the solar calendar, meaning that they fall on the same day every year, unlike Ramadan and other religious observances (marked with an asterisk) that follow a lunar calendar and change from year to year.

* Martyrdom of Imam Ali
* Eid al-Fitr (End of Ramadan)
* Martyrdom of Imam Ja'far Sadeq
* Birthday of Imam Reza
  February 11 Magnificent Victory of the Islamic Revolution Day
* Eid al-Adha (Feast of the Sacrifice)
* Eid Ghadir Khom
  March 20 Oil Nationalization Day
  March 21–24 Now Ruz (New Year)
  April 1 Islamic Republic Day
  April 2 Sizdeh Bedar (Public Outing Day)
  April 5 Anniversary of 1963 Uprising
* Tasu'a
* Ashoura
* Arba'een (Martyrdom of Imam Hussain)
  June 4 Death of Khomeini
  June 5 Anniversary of Uprising Against the shah
* Mouloud (the Prophet's birthday)/ Imam Ja'far Sedeq's birthday
* Death of the Prophet
* Birthday of Imam Ali
* Leilat al-Meiraj (Ascension of the Prophet)
* Birthday of Imam Mahdi
* Beginning of Ramadan

Iranian women jump over a raging fire to celebrate the ancient festival called Shab-e-chahar Shanbeh Suri on the eve of the last Wednesday of the Iranian calendar. The fire festival is believed to date back to 1725 BC when Zoroastrianism was the predominant religion of ancient Persia. During this night, people gather on the streets in their neighborhoods or in their backyards. The flames represent the triumph of good over evil, while jumping over the fire removes the presence of evil. Lighting fire was considered a sacred Zoroastrian blessing. Small children, often covered to hide their identities, go door to door banging pots with spoons to receive treats.

Iranians—and other Shiite Muslims worldwide—consider Hussein's death to be so horrific, a dramatic and public mourning often marks its anniversary.

Hussein was the grandson of Muhammad and a crucial figure for Shiite Muslims. In AD 680, he was killed along with thousands of his followers during the Battle at Karbala by warriors sent by the Umayyad caliph Yazid I. This further deepened anger and misunderstanding between Sunni and Shiite Muslims.

To mark Hussein's death, modern Shiites march through the streets of Iran beating themselves with chains, piercing their skin with needles and hooks, and reciting stories of his sacrifice. Others will wear only black or dark-colored clothing (red is forbidden).

Ashura, on the tenth day of this month, marks the moment of his death and becomes particularly passionate. No weddings or parties are held during Muharram, and many wealthy Iranians donate money to the poor in Hussein's honor at this time. Iranians also honor Hussein's memory in passion plays known as *Ta'ziyeh*.

National Holidays

Iran's national holidays commemorate more recent political events. On February 11, the country celebrates Magnificent Victory of the Islamic Revolution, which marks the day the shah was driven into exile and the Ayatollah Khomeini came to power. In Tehran, the ten days leading up to this holiday are often filled with concerts of military music and cultural events.

In April, two holidays are set aside to celebrate Iran's national strength. They are Revolution Day

A Muslim woman offers dates to a woman and her child at the Imam Khomeini Mosque during Eid al-Fitr. A picture of Iran's late founder of the Islamic Revolution, Ayatollah Ruhollah Khomeini, hangs in the background. A very important aspect of Eid, a day of joy and thanks, is the charity that all Muslims are expected to extend to the needy. It is believed that the Koran was revealed to Muhammad during Shawaal, the lunar month when Eid takes place.

and Islamic Republic Day, both of which fill the streets with marchers carrying banners with life-sized pictures of both Ayatollahs Khomeini and Khamenie. Heart Rending Departure of the Great Leader of the Islamic Republic of Iran is June 4 and marks Khomeini's death of a heart attack in 1989. This holiday is extremely important to Iranians, who take to the streets dressed in funeral garb to publicly mourn their former leader.

Weddings

While some elements of marriage have changed since Iran became an Islamic nation, the wedding ceremony itself has remained steeped in ancient Persian traditions. Marriage is not celebrated without fanfare. There are normally two stages to the ceremony, much like Western traditions, starting with the *aghed* (ceremony), where the couple is bound together legally, followed by a celebration, which will often last several days to a week, a much shorter celebration than in ancient times.

By custom, the aghed and the reception party that follows usually take place at the home of the bride. The imam performs the ceremony, which consists of readings and recitations from the Koran and then the signing of a marriage contract and the *mahr*, which is the official "bride price" to guarantee the couple's financial security.

The bride is then asked three times if she agrees to the marriage. She only answers after the third time. This is to signify that it is the husband

The Iranian brides in this photograph are in line for a mass wedding ceremony of 1,000 couples. Marriage is seen as a civil contract between Islamic men and women, often with the husband agreeing to support his wife and family. Married couples in Iran do not share their property, but women can maintain financial independence. Iranian women are allowed to marry one man at a time and must wait three months after divorce or childbirth before remarrying.

who desires her and not the other way around. During the ceremony, relatives of the couple hold a scarf over their heads. Two pieces of crystallized sugar are rubbed together, which is a symbolic act "to sweeten" the couple's future. At the same time, two different parts of the fabric are sewn together over the heads of the couple to signify their union. In a traditional Zoroastrian ceremony, a tray is held over the groom's head that holds two pieces of cloth sewn together, scissors, a raw egg, a piece of fruit (apple or pomegranate), some dried marjoram, and sweetmeats.

THE RELIGIONS OF IRAN THROUGHOUT ITS HISTORY

6

In the days before the Persian Empire, the Aryans who migrated to central Asia worshiped elements of nature, such as fire and water, and celestial bodies, such as the moon and sun. Any practice of worshiping more than one element or god for religious purposes is called polytheism ("poly" meaning more than one, "theism" meaning belief in a god or gods).

By 1000 BC, this worship of nature developed into the Zoroastrian religion, which originated from the region of present-day Azerbaijan. It was there that the prophet Zoroaster (also known as Zarathushtra) was born. He soon arrived in the city of Pars, then the heart of the Achaemenid dynasty. In 522 BC, King Darius I become the first Persian to convert to Zoroastrianism.

Zoroastrianism is one of the world's oldest religions and is still practiced today. It came about in a time before Persians used the written word, and for many hundreds of years the followers of Zoroaster passed their beliefs down by word of mouth. This is the reason why there are so few written testaments of this religion. But during the beginning of the sixth century BC, a collection of holy texts called the Avesta was recorded in a specially invented alphabet. It was a compilation of twenty-one books

Built between AD 1602 and 1618, the Sheikh Lotfollah Mosque *(left)* was dedicated to Shah Abbas's father-in-law, Sheikh Lotfollah. Compared to many other mosques in Iran, the Sheikh Lotfollah Mosque is relatively small but is no less magnificent. Depending on the lighting, its dome changes color from cream to pink. A Persian coin *(above)* from the second century BC depicts a Zoroastrian fire altar. Ancient Persia began producing coins around 546 BC and was the first culture to issue coins depicting portraits of leaders.

Zoroastrians read their holy book, the Avesta, at the Pir-e-Herisht Temple during the Sadeh festival in Ardakan. The Sadeh, or the feast of the creation of fire, has been celebrated by Zoroastrians since ancient times. Devout Zoroastrians must pray five times a day and in the presence of a flame, which is considered a symbol of order and justice.

and not attributed to any author, unlike the Bible and Torah, where each chapter is attributed to a specific prophet. All original copies of the Avesta were destroyed during the many invasions of Persia.

The basis of the Zoroastrian religion was its duality of good and evil. Varying forces such as fire and light, or darkness represented Ahura Mazda, the Zoroastrian god. Other well-known religious ideologies such as a person's free choice to act in either good or evil ways, resurrection, redemption, final judgment, and the idea of a heaven or paradise—a word that has its origins in Old Persian—originated with Zoroastrianism.

Susa and Persepolis were the sites of the greatest Zoroastrian temples, where caretakers kept giant fires burning at all times. These fires

The wall ruins pictured in this photograph were once a part of an Elamite settlement in Susa, the site of one of the oldest settlements in the Middle East. Between 4000 and 2000 BC, Susa was a flourishing civilization that claimed to be the capital of the world. Archaeologists have been excavating the extensive remains of Susa for well over a century.

represented the followers' respect for Ahura. Ahura also figures predominately in the creation myth of Persia, as set down in the *Bundahishn*. These stories are similar to biblical creation stories of how man was created and then corrupted by evil. But because Zoroastrianism originated before Judaism and Christianity, the Persians were the first civilization to believe in a monotheistic religion. Many scholars believe that this religion was a great source of inspiration to future monotheistic doctrines.

Zoroaster, believed to have lived to the age of seventy-seven, was killed by local villagers for criticizing their religious beliefs and performing ritual animal sacrifices. Zoroastrianism held strong until about AD 650 when Arabs, who were followers of Islam, began invading Persia. A number of Zoroastrians then fled to India, where modern followers of the religion are referred to as Parsees.

The History of Islam

During the early seventh century AD, in a city called Mecca, an Arab merchant named Muhammad began having a series of intense visions. He experienced these revelations as he traveled throughout the Arabian desert. From these visions, he and his followers began a new religion called Islam, which means "submission to the will of God (or Allah)" in Arabic. After Muhammad's death, the messages and visions he received were recorded as the teachings of Islam in a book called the Koran.

Islam is the youngest of the world's major religions, which include Judaism, Christianity, and Buddhism. It is closely

This manuscript page represents the opening page of the Koran's first *sura*, or chapter. The Koran is comprised of 114 suras and is believed to be the word of Allah as dictated to the prophet Muhammad over a twenty-three-year span.

This illustration of a Zoroastrian worshiper praying before a small fire altar in Baku appeared in the *Illustrated London News* in 1885. Zoroastrians do not worship fire, as is often believed. For Zoroastrians, fire is simply a symbol of the power of their god, Ahura Mazda.

related to Jewish and Christian faiths for its sharing of many of the same prophets such as Jesus and Moses. It is also similar to Zoroastrianism in that it is a monotheistic faith. Along with the Koran, there is a book of Islamic customs called the *Sunna* (or *Sunnah*), which is used to help formulate Islamic law (*sharia*, or *shar'ia*).

During Muhammad's lifetime, Islam began to spread across central Asia. After his death in AD 632, Muslims migrated to other countries and established Islamic empires, which eventually stretched from central Asia to Spain. At the beginning of the twenty-first century there were more than one billion practicing Muslims in the world, or about 20 percent of the world's faithful.

When Arab warriors conquered the Sassanids in the seventh century, Iran became an Arab-Muslim empire. Although Zoroastrians, Jews, and Christians were allowed to follow their individual faiths, they were charged a *jizyah* (tax) in order to do so. Although some Persians became Muslims in order to avoid this tax, many others embraced Islamic beliefs because they promised more equality than did Zoroastrianism, which relied on a strict class system. Muslims recognized the importance of the individual, even as they somewhat forcefully imposed their will over the Persians.

The Changing Face of Islam

At the time of Muhammad's death in AD 632, his son-in-law Ali was living in Persia and was believed by some Muslims to be the next true leader, or imam. But the world's majority of Muslims elected another caliph to lead them. The minority who opposed this election became known as *shi'ah* of Ali, which means "friend of Ali." This group became known as Shia, and the members of this sect are known as Shiite Muslims.

Shiites remain the predominate sect of modern Muslims in Iran. Shiites believe that each of the successive supreme leaders should be a descendant of the original prophet, while Sunni Muslims believe in appointing a new leader from qualified clerics. The main difference between Shiite and Sunni Muslims is who they believe is their religious leader. Most of the world's Muslim population is Sunni (about 85 percent), while Shiites make up only a small percentage of Muslims.

All Muslims accept that there is only one god, Allah, and that the Koran is the direct word of Allah. The Koran outlines guidelines for all aspects of Muslim life, including moral and ethical behavior, marriage, divorce, inheritance, social life, and diet. The *Sunna* contains all the known sayings of Muhammad and his feelings on philosophical and legal questions. The Koran and *Sunna* are used as the source of all Islamic laws, which have evolved only slightly over the centuries. Used together, they are the basis for Islamic society. Although Islamic beliefs claim not to recognize a pecking order of authority, there are learned men called the imams, caliphs, ayatollah, and *ulema* (the plural of *mullah*), who are the unquestionable political, social, and spiritual leaders. They are charged with the responsibility of interpreting the laws of Islam for all people.

The Five Pillars of Islam

Following is a list of the five essential practices that each Muslim must observe:

1. The belief *(shahada)* that there is no god but Allah, and Muhammad is his prophet.

2. The obligation of praying *(salat)* five times a day toward Mecca.

3. The obligation of giving alms *(zakat)*, meaning charitable contributions; to share one's blessings.

4. The obligation of fasting during the month of Ramadan to feel the pain of the disadvantaged and develop self-discipline.

5. The pilgrimage *(hajj)* that every adult Muslim has to undertake to Mecca, provided he or she is physically and financially able to do so, to have a sense of community and to exchange ideas.

This illustration depicts Muhammad's son-in-law, Ali, who Shiite Muslims believe to be Muhammad's successor. The largest Shiite sect is known as the Twelver Shiites, which refers to Ali's successors of imams. The Twelvers believe that the position of imam was passed down from Ali to eleven of his family members. The twelfth and final imam was born in AD 868 and went into hiding. Shiites believe that he lives and waits to return.

Islam Today

Since the revolution in 1979, religion is the driving force behind every aspect of Iranian life. In fact, because Iran is a religious state, Islamic laws, as interpreted by the current ayatollah, Ali Khamenei, determine everything that affects an Iranian's life. Iran's current president, Mohammad Khatami, has no control over police, courts, or the military. Khatami's influence is primarily that of a governmental figurehead, although he does have a voice in certain legislation and also meets regularly with the ayatollah. While Khatami, who was first elected in 1997, is more moderate than his predecessor Akbar Rafsanjani, who was a very strict cleric, he has been hard-pressed to make any major societal changes.

Because the majority of Iran's population is under the age of thirty, the election of Khatami, who is considered to be a strong reformist, seemed to be a signal of a more liberal administration. Iranian youths are hoping to loosen the extreme Islamic laws that bind every facet of an Iranian's life.

To people who were born after the 1979 revolution and who have been exposed to more worldly views and Western ideas, Iran's lifestyle restrictions have largely become frustrating. Khatami has dramatically enforced traditional laws with new security forces patrolling city streets in search of what he deems as "moral corruption." Popular music, for example, is condemned as a distraction from the service of Allah. Dancing, especially between men and women, is considered corrupt and sinful. These behaviors, and others like them, are considered morally dangerous. Strict punishments are often administered for acts such as smoking or drinking alcoholic

beverages. Committing acts of homosexuality is punishable by death. Adultery can bring about stoning, while kissing in public is worthy of one hundred lashes with a whip.

All of these rules are meant to keep Iranians focused on the importance of their religion by removing external distractions. Each day is instead structured around time for prayer and contemplation. Muslims are required to pray facing Mecca five times a day, in the early morning, in the early noon, in the late afternoon, at sunset, and at night.

Other Religions

Sufism is a minor Islamic sect. Sufis also follow the Koran but focus instead on extreme levels of spirituality. The Sufis believe that it is impossible to prove the existence of Allah and that a person can only feel Allah's presence as a light that shines in the purest of hearts. In order to purify one's heart and be united

Muslims in this photograph pray during Friday prayers on the first day of Ramadan, a month-long Islamic observance that begins during the ninth month of the Islamic lunar calendar. A lunar calendar uses the moon instead of the sun to determine the passage of time. The thin crescent of a new moon indicates the beginning of festivities, often signaled by the phrase *"Ramadan Mubarak,"* meaning "Have a blessed and happy Ramadan." In addition to fasting for a month, Muslims also refrain from arguing, fighting, lying, and speaking ill of others. Ramadan is a time to practice self-control and resolve past arguments.

Women and Islam

The revolution of 1979 also brought about a huge impact on women's freedoms. They were once again ordered to veil themselves and wear the traditional chador, or long cloak. Many women who had previously been working during the time of the shahs were now ordered home to fulfill the holy duty of motherhood. Women's legal rights were also affected, with a mother having no say over her children's upbringing and a wife not protected by law from a violent husband. A man could also order his wife out of the house or divorce her without any explanation or recourse.

with Allah, Sufis must follow a path to a higher consciousness, often giving up material goods in order to achieve this state. A small percentage of Sufis live in Iran, although most reside in India.

The Ghulat are an extreme sect of the Shiite faith. They are highly secretive and often practice their ceremonies in seclusion to avoid attention. They consider men's moustaches extremely important based on a legend. As the story goes, the early prophet Imam Ali bowed down to Muhammad and brushed his moustache against him, thereby making facial hair sacred. No Ghulat ever trims or shaves his moustache.

The Sufi man seen in this photograph holds prayer beads. Sufism is a mystical sect of Islam that teaches its followers to move toward the truth by means of love and devotion. Sufis believe the only way to become perfect is to purify oneself under the training of a perfect Sufi master. Sufism was founded in the fourteenth century by Shah Nimatullah Wali, considered one of Persia's greatest Sufi masters, though Sufis recognize Muhammad as the first Sufi.

This thirteenth-century illustration, located in the Armenian Cathedral in Isfahan, depicts Jesus Christ washing the feet of a disciple. Iran's indigenous population of Christians currently includes an estimated 250,000 Armenians, 32,000 Assyrians, and a small population of Roman Catholics, Protestants, and Anglicans, who were converted by missionaries in the nineteenth and twentieth centuries. Armenians comprise the largest Christian community in Iran and are concentrated mainly in its major cities.

The Baha'i religion was begun in the nineteenth century by an Iranian religious cleric named Mizra Ali Mohammed. He called himself the Bab, which means "gate." His follower, Mizra Husain Ali, converted many believers and was considered a prophet on the same level as Jesus, Muhammad, Zoroaster, and Buddha.

In Baha'i there are no ceremonies or sacraments. Followers of this faith are critical of the legal inequalities of the sexes in traditional Islam and feel that religion must adapt to serve its time. Since Iran's 1979 revolution, the Baha'i faith has been prohibited, although some of its followers still live in the Iranian countryside.

There is a large Christian community of Armenians in the Jolfa district of Isfahan. They have their own cathedral and are allowed to celebrate a traditional Sunday mass. Another Christian religious center is St. Thaddeus, a fortified monastery in nearby Azerbaijan. Thousands of Iranian Christians make a pilgrimage to the St. Thaddeus monastery every July.

Iran is also home to a very small Jewish population. Since the 1979 revolution, many Jews have left the country, but there are some communities that still exist. While followers of minority religions have recently been allowed certain freedoms and representation in the parliament (Majlis), they are expected to observe all Islamic public codes of conduct.

THE ART AND ARCHITECTURE OF IRAN

7

Today Iran is respected as a leader in the arts, due mainly to the Persian traditions of working with textiles, fabrics, ceramics, metals, and woods. They were also renowned gardeners, motivating some historians to consider that landscape gardening was an idea that originated with the Persians and dates as far back as Cyrus the Great.

At their height, Persian artistic achievements are considered some of the world's greatest examples of miniature painting and woven carpets. Many modern Iranians also keep these arts alive by working in traditional methods much like their earlier ancestors did.

Persian Architecture

Much of the earliest Persian architecture dates from the time of Darius I, also known as Darius the Great, who reigned between 522 and 486 BC and was a champion of the arts. He built the city of Persepolis, which today is in ruins. Persepolis— once an ancient city of kings' palaces and tombs— now reveals clues to the amazing buildings of the time. Fire temples and altars reflecting the beliefs of the Zoroastrians, whose reverence of fire as holy, were prominently featured as a

In 1971, the shah of Iran built the famous Azadi Tower, or Freedom Tower *(left)*, in Tehran for the 2,500th anniversary of the Persian Empire. The building, a combination of traditional and Western styles, also houses an underground museum. On the very top of the building is a moon rock brought back by the U.S. astronauts of *Apollo 11* and given to the shah by former U.S. president Richard M. Nixon (1913–1994). The ancient city of Persepolis, seen in ruins *(above)*, was begun around 518 BC and completed a century later. Before buildings could be erected, considerable work on the city's foundation needed to take place, including cutting into the irregular and rocky mountainside.

This aerial view of Isfahan shows its historic Imam Khomeini Square and the surrounding city. The square was built in 1612 under the reign of Shah Abbas I and covers an area that measures 1,640 feet by 525 feet (500 by 160 meters). It is near two of Iran's most distinguished houses of worship, the Imam Mosque and the Sheikh Lotfollah Mosque. Isfahan, once considered the jewel of ancient Persia, is still one of Iran's most beloved cities. During the Safavid dynasty, Abbas made Isfahan his capital, and the Persians who lived in its environs produced some of the most beautiful architecture and art of the period.

part of these structures. Darius considered Persepolis his capital. For more than a century, artists from all over the empire were brought to Persepolis in order to work their magic.

Most structures were made of stone, but over time, oven- and sun-baked bricks became the common building materials. In fact, brick was first invented in Iran. Artists then began molding or carving these bricks with decorative designs. By AD 700, Islam had a profound effect on the architecture of Iran, with beautiful temples built for worship. These temples are notable for their spectacular domes, many of which are covered in glazed blue tiles. Muslims also built palaces, religious schools called *madrassas*, bridges, baths, and remarkable gardens often with running streams.

Shah Abbas I, in the early 1600s during the Safavid dynasty, advanced Islamic art and architecture immensely when he built Isfahan, a city that became the capital of his empire.

Isfahan's Khaju Bridge stretches 433 feet (132 meters) and has twenty-three stone arches. It was built in 1650 by Shah Abbas II and originally functioned as a dam. The Khaju has two levels, the lower of which regulated the flow of the Zayandeh River. Abbas had a center pavilion built on the Khaju, complete with seats carved from stone to enjoy the view.

Today, Isfahan remains a city where one can view Iran's past. It is an attractive and unusual city, and one highly sought after by international tourists to see beautiful Persian architecture. Shah Abbas commissioned Iman (Royal) Square (sometimes referred to as Khomeini Square), an enormous twenty-acre open space in the center of the city that served as polo and parade grounds. Several splendid palaces also remain as a testament to Abbas's architectural commitments, including the Palace of Chehel Sotun (the Forty Columns Palace, so-called because its reflection in surrounding waters doubles its twenty columns to forty). He also erected the Masjid-i-Shah, or Royal Mosque, the Friday Mosque, the gates of the Great Bazaar, and two remarkable arched bridges over the Zayandeh River.

Muslim Architecture

The influence of Islamic architecture in Iran is primarily seen in its houses of worship. The mosque is the official place of prayer, although Muslims, when called to pray, are only required to face Mecca and can therefore perform their prayers anywhere. The mosque is an open structure with a

This ceramic star-shaped tile dates from between the thirteenth and fourteenth century. One of the oldest forms of Persian art is pottery, with artifacts now being found that date back to the fifth millennium BC. Beginning in the ninth century, Persia's ornate and colorful pottery became famous around the world. During the Mongol period, Chinese influences dominated Persian works until the mid-eighteenth century.

The Masjid-i Shah, or Royal Mosque, is considered the crowning architectural achievement of Shah Abbas I. However, he didn't live to see its completion. Construction of the mosque began in 1611 and utilized an estimated eighteen million bricks and 472,500 tiles. The mosque is celebrated for its colorful tile work in blue, yellow, turquoise, pink, purple, and green.

covered sanctuary that houses a prayer niche directing worshipers to face Mecca. The mosque also has a minaret (an outdoor ledge) from which the faithful are called by the *muezzin*, the crier who calls Muslims to their daily prayer.

The dome of a mosque rises high towards the heavens and is usually covered with tiles that sparkle in sunlight and can be seen from a distance. Persian architects engineered methods of building domes using fewer support columns, thereby keeping the inner areas of the mosques open. They also learned how to use the desert winds to keep the buildings cool.

Miniature Painting

Beginning in the fourteenth century, the Safavid dynasty (1501–1722) had a great

This sixteenth-century miniature painting depicts a royal hunt. Art completed in this style flourished in Islamic Persia from the fourteenth to the seventeenth centuries. An art form that utilized brilliant colors, masterful brushwork, and Arabic calligraphy, paintings of this sort are often found in royal manuscripts. Only the rich and powerful could afford manuscripts, as materials to make them were very expensive and usually included gold and silver leaf.

influence on Persian art and is sometimes referred to as its Golden Age. In keeping with the importance of literature in Iranian history, miniature book illustration became the focus of most artwork of this period. Cities such as Herat (now in Afghanistan) became artistic centers, producing many such artists. Later groups of miniature painters also emerged in Tabriz and Bukhara. These artists specialized in colorful detailed paintings that depicted lush landscapes, beautiful gardens, and portraiture of warriors, magicians, and princesses, many following popular stories of the day. The *Book of Kings* itself contains nearly 300 such works.

Later, plant and animal images became popular as well as the human form, depicted quite sensuously by the sixteenth century, thanks in part to European influences.

Although strict translation of Islamic law forbids the painting of human or animal images, Iran's Shiite Muslims rejected this rule, and in Iran the Koran is brightly illustrated with miniatures translating the holy stories.

After the revolution in 1979, a trend toward more realistic painting began. Today, paintings show a more realistic side of human interaction, though many retain a strong influence for imaginary themes.

Crafts

Many examples of ancient pottery were excavated from the city of Khorasan in Iran and traced back to 6000 BC. Brightly painted bowls and vases were covered with a clear glaze that preserved their designs. Metalwork has also survived as an example of Iran's rich artistry. Many relics contain Arabic inscriptions ranging from wishes for good luck and health to religious proverbs. Gold, silver, and valuable gems

The Naderi Throne (*naderi* means "rare" or "unique") is one of the three thrones of Iran. It can be taken apart into twelve sections since it was required that it be moved to various royal residences. Constructed of wood and covered in gold and jewels, it is 7.5 feet (2.2 meters) in height. Engraved designs include a peacock's tail on the backrest, ducks, dragons, leaves, tree branches, and a lion on the footstool.

When Cyrus the Great conquered Babylon, he was struck by the splendor of handwoven carpets, such as the sixteenth-century Indo-Persian carpet seen in this photograph. It was actually Cyrus who is credited with introducing carpet weaving to ancient Persia, an art form that reached its pinnacle during the sixteenth century. Historical records show that Persian carpets decorated the court and eventually the tomb of Cyrus the Great.

were often used to assemble ornate jewelry. In fact, three of Iran's most valued treasures are its thrones, which are inlaid with thousands of precious and semiprecious gemstones.

Hand-woven Persian carpets are world-renowned for their beauty and symbolism. They were not woven as floor coverings, but as works of art to hang on the walls. Often depicting magical scenes of epic battles or visions of paradise, carpet weaving began when nomadic Turks brought these skills from central Asia. During the Sassanid dynasty, Chosroes II created a carpet for his palace that was amazing in its realism. It showed an exotic garden filled with trees and flowers. Its streams were represented by gold and silver threads, while precious stones and silk were used to create its gardens. It was the most expensive carpet in history. During the Arabic invasions, it was cut into small pieces so it could be carried away.

In the renaissance period of Shah Abbas I, the art of carpet weaving became a national

The Persians were the pioneer carpet weavers of the medieval world, achieving an extraordinary degree of ingenuity in both skill and creativity. Woven carpets evolved from simple articles to protect nomadic tribesmen from the damp floor to possessions marking the wealth and prestige of kings and noblemen.

The History of Calligraphy

Calligraphy, or writing in an elaborate script, has its beginnings in the cave paintings of early Egypt. Stylized writing began with the invention of hieroglyphics in 3500 BC. Calligraphy is highly regarded by Iranians, especially because they so respect the written word. Because Muslims believe that Allah taught man to write, it is therefore considered a wonderful religious journey to write passages from the Koran in Arabic using calligraphy. There are six major scripts in Arabic calligraphy. They are Farsi, Naskh, Kufi, Deewani, Reqíaa, and Thuluth, all of which represent various artistic styles.

industry. Although Persian carpets are currently made in India, Pakistan, and Turkey, each country has a distinctive design and color scheme so that an expert can always tell an Iranian carpet from one woven elsewhere. In Iran, the colors of the dye used in Persian carpets hold specific meanings. The color white, for instance, means mourning, grief, or death; black means destruction; orange means devotion and piety; red means happiness or health; and brown means fertility.

Sixteenth- and seventeenth-century designs most often depicted scenes of paradise, commonly associated with beautiful

This man works at his cloth workshop in Isfahan. The skill of carpet weaving is handed down from father to son as a closely guarded secret. Today, carpet weaving is the most popular and widespread handicraft in Iran. Persian carpets are still renowned for their richness of color, variety of patterns, and quality of designs.

gardens. This idea is based on the Koran's vision of paradise as a garden filled with lush fruit, rippling streams, sweet-smelling flowers, shady trees, and beautiful attendants. Persian carpets may also include geometric shapes and Arabic lettering. Although many modern carpets are machine-woven to meet consumers' demands, quite a few modern weavers continue to create handmade carpets.

Performing Arts

In ancient Persia, many types of plays were performed for royalty. The Middle Ages continued to offer Persian theater in the form of Ta'ziyeh, religious dramas of the sixteenth century. Usually these passion plays are spoken in verse and are the only classical form of Persian drama where the text was written. At weddings and special occasions, comical skits were performed. *Baqqaal-baazi*, *ruhawzi* or *takht hawzi* were performed over courtyard pools that were covered with boards to make a stage. *Siaah-baazi* were comedies where the main character wore blackface. *Khiaal-bazi* used shadows to convey a story, and *khayma-shap-baazi* was a marionette show, while *ëaruasak-baazi* or *ëaruasak-e posht-e parda* involved the use of puppets. The standard plots of these skits revolved around lovers' quarrels or the relationship between the rich and the poor. They were generally improvised, depending on the plot, and were never written down.

In the nineteenth century, when wealthy Persians went overseas, they became acquainted with Western theater. In the beginning, Western plays were mainly translated into Persian and performed only at court. Over the years, however, Iranian writers created their own Western-influenced works with themes having much to do with government corruption and social problems.

In 1911, a national theater was formed in Tehran. During the 1920s, the time of Reza Shah, plays that criticized the government were strictly censored. But after his abdication in 1941, there was a period of artistic freedom in Iran. An opportunity arose for Iranian artists to become acquainted with dramatists from all over the world. Writers and actors began to express their own thoughts on the state of humanity without fear of being censored. During the final years of the last shah, however, policies that enforced censorship were again employed, and any production critical of the government was shut down.

Devout Muslims felt that Western influences produced plays that were sinful. After the revolution in 1979, many actors and writers fled Iran to escape persecution. Dramatic performances began to be used as a tool for religious and state propaganda with content that reflected only the values of the Islamic regime. Because of dress codes and limited interaction between men and women, performances were much more restricted. By the late 1980s, there were about one hundred government-supported theatrical troupes, much like there are today.

Cinema

Film production in Iran dates back to the early 1930s when silent comedies in Iran made their debut. By 1934, the first "talkie" called *The Lor Girl* was made in India by a former resident of Iran. During World War II, film production came to a halt, only to resume in 1949 with melodramas and comedies made purely for entertainment.

In the 1970s, an Iranian film movement called the New Wave was born. It focused on new aspiring Iranian filmmakers whose art produced films of social consciousness. Although supported by a worldwide following, the Iranian government consistently censored these filmmakers, thereby forcing them to use symbolic and metaphoric depictions. Several New Wave filmmakers continue their work today, including Bahram Beyzaie.

After 1979, hundreds of theaters were razed by Islamic fundamentalists who thought movies were agents of moral corruption. Many filmmakers were arrested on charges of "corrupting the public." More than 2,000 previously shown domestic and foreign films were then reviewed by the ministers of culture and only a few hundred received clearance to be seen again in Iran.

Some films had to be drastically edited to meet strict government standards. Many restrictions had to do with the way women were represented on screen.

Despite the restrictions, Iranian movie production has been steadily rising since President Khatami's election. Sixty to seventy Iranian films debut annually, many to great fanfare overseas.

THE LITERATURE AND MUSIC OF IRAN

8

Perhaps Iran's greatest cultural legacy lies in its poetry. Dating back to the court poets of Persia, Iran has been home to the greatest number of poets per capita than in any other place in the world. Many examples of Persian poetry, including a few that date to the ninth century BC, are preserved today. They range from *qasidas*, which are formal odes (tribute poems) to *ghazals*, which are love poems. Poetry came into its national renown in the eleventh century AD when Firdawsi wrote his epic *Shahnameh*. This astounding work was written in 60,000 couplets and told of both mythical kings and historically accurate figures in early Persian history. At the time of its writing, it was illustrated by Persia's most famous artists.

In the tenth century lived a poet named Omar Khayyam (1048–1122), who wrote the *Rubáiyat* and was one of the most revered writers of his time. He was also a skilled mathematician and astronomer, who successfully mapped the Persian lunar and solar calendars. Many scholars feel that to fully appreciate the *Rubáiyat*, it must be read in its original language of Persian, although its translation became very popular with nineteenth-century English readers.

The poet and prophet Mevlâna Jalaluddîn Rumi (1207–1273; also known as Mowlana or Mowlavi in Iran and

The Sufi poet Mevlâna Jalaluddîn Rumi (1207–1273), pictured in this illustration *(above)*, is considered one of the greatest Persian poets of all time. His book, *Masnawi*, is sometimes called the Persian Koran. One day, he repeated Allah's name in ecstasy and later began to hear the name of Allah in every sound and began to whirl. Later he founded the Mevlevi Sufi order, Sufis that became known as the Whirling Dervishes. This seventeenth-century Persian illumination *(left)* depicts a palace garden.

Indian and Iranian government officials in this photograph stand in front of the tomb of the Persian poet Shams-ud-din-Muhammad, popularly known as Hafiz. Hafiz was a master of ode, couplet, and short lyric poems but is renowned for his *ghazals*, or love sonnets. Ghazals are considered the soul of Persian lyric poetry, which portrays deep human insights through beautiful language.

Turkey) lived in the thirteenth century. He was a devout Sufi Muslim who wrote in a mystical style that gained him a great following. He traveled throughout the Middle East on horseback, all the while having religious visions that he wrote down in verse. His other poems were self-reflective or were whimsical observations on life and love.

Shams-ud-din-Muhammad, more popularly known as Hafiz, was also a Sufi Muslim poet. He lived from 1325 to 1389 and was said to have memorized the entire Koran. During his lifetime, he wrote more than 700 lyric poems, many featuring devotional themes. Others told stories of adventures and visions. Most of all, Hafiz's poetry is a celebration of life and of living itself. Though religious in nature, and hundreds of years old, it continues to resonate worldwide, especially in Iran, where copies of his books are always among the nation's top sellers. Hafiz's tomb in Shiraz has become a place of pilgrimage for Iranians and foreign travelers alike. Followers read his passionate verses and feel that they are as moving and contemporary today as they were hundreds of years ago.

Modern Literature

While poetry was the major form of literary expression in early Persian writings, short stories and prose began to flourish with the release of *Golestan* (*The Rose*

Garden) written by Saídi in the thirteenth century. His style was known as *hekaayaat* (anecdotal), usually revolving around a moral point and having to do with a character like a scholar or a king.

At the turn of the century, short stories became more popular because writers like Ali Akbar Dehkhoda, Mohammad Ali Jamalzadeh, and Sadegh Hedayat wrote in a straightforward style that could be easily understood by ordinary people. *Hedayatís Buf I Kur* (The Blind Owl), for example, was the first Iranian book to use the speech and mannerisms of working people.

Engaging the reader in current issues made Iranian literature even more provocative. Since reading had always been important to Iranians, nineteenth- and twentieth-century writers used literature to increase the world's awareness of Iran's social issues and problems. This movement to social realism caused many writers to face persecution by the government if the opinions they expressed were unpopular.

> Rise up nimbly
> And go on your strange journey
> To the ocean of meanings.
> The stream knows
> It can't stay on the mountain.
> Leave and don't look away
> From the sun as you go
> In whose light
> You're sometimes crescent,
> Sometimes full.
>
> —Rumi (1207–1273),
> excerpt translated from Persian by
> Coleman Barks

Pictured here is one page of a Persian manuscript that dates back to the Islamic Empire. Since the end of the nineteenth century, prose has achieved a greater importance in Iran's literary history. Modern prose has enabled storytellers and novelists to engage readers' attention in social and political issues of Iran. However, due to the nature of the subject matter presented, many Iranian writers are subjected to censorship or forced into exile.

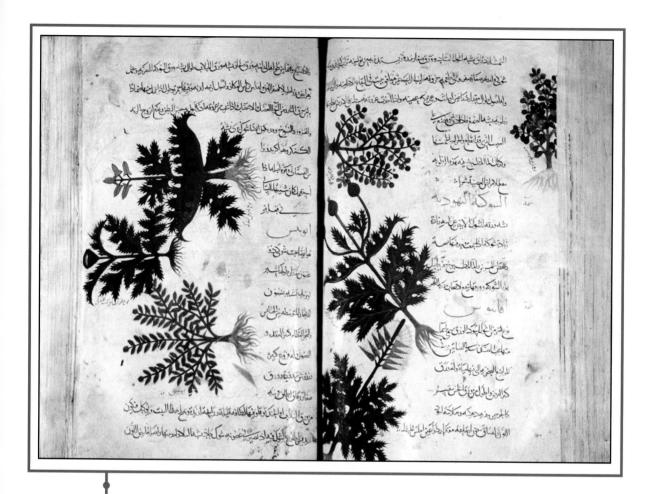

Pictured on these pages is an Arabic edition of Greek physician Pedanius Dioscoride's book, *The Materials of Medicine*. The manuscript, which dates from AD 50 to 70, categorizes more than 1,000 natural drugs, largely derived from plants, though some also come from animals and minerals. Dioscoride's work was read by generations of healers after his death in AD 90, as the basis for their pharmacological instruction.

During the Pahlavi dynasty, right before the 1979 Islamic Revolution, many poets and writers spent years in prison because of their opinions. Others fled the country creating a movement of authors-in-exile who continued to use the traditional Persian language. This work, often smuggled into Iran on the so-called black market, enjoys great popularity among Iranians. Much of this fiction is nostalgic for the writers' homeland while remaining honest about Iran's political arena.

A literary revolution began with the return of the Ayatollah Khomeini in 1979 and the strict fundamentalism of Islamic traditions that followed. At that time, most writers were focused on methods to continue publishing their work while redefining its tone. Many authors went into exile when pressure from the Islamic Republic of Iran began suppressing their work. Others acted independently and had their work published underground with great success.

Traditional Music

Persian music traditionally focused on the poetry of the lyrics rather than the melody, which was often very simple. Historians have found that the lute, an Arabic instrument that looks like a guitar, was one of the first instruments used in the eighth and ninth centuries as the Islamic Empire moved into Iran. Others include a *nay*, or bamboo flute; a *santur*, a stringed instrument that you lay on your lap like a zither; an *ud*, an Arabic lute with a rounder belly and a shorter neck; a *sitar*, a three-stringed instrument; a *chang*, or harp; and a *daira*, or tambourine. Drums are also used frequently.

While Arabic instruments influenced Persian music, the Persian love of poetry in turn influenced the Arabic sound and so was born traditional Iranian music. Mysticism was also an important element of early Persian music, and early pieces were often focused around the singing of hymns. The songs can be mournful or mesmerizing mainly because of the vocal gymnastics of the singer and the lyrics that he or she is singing.

This manuscript illumination depicts a music scene in a Persian court of royalty. Throughout its history, Persian music has influenced and been influenced by Greeks, Arabs, and Indians. After Islam became established in Persia, a musician's importance depended upon the views of the current leader. Depending on the period, musicians themselves were sometimes condemned by Islamic society. One of the most popular forms of acceptable music was the singing of the Koran's verses. Scholars believe this is the reason why vocals are the cornerstone of traditional Persian music.

Humay and Humayun are seen in a garden feasting among musicians in this Persian manuscript illumination that dates from 1396. Persian musicians often inspired poets who were influenced by the rhythm and form of the music, oftentimes instigating improvisational techniques. However, Persian improvisation drastically differs from the free improvisation utilized by jazz musicians living in Western countries. Improvisation in Persian music involves following rules and requires the musician to internalize the ancient melodies in a style known as *radif*. Until a decade ago, radif was preserved through oral traditions passed down from master to student.

Music has traditionally been reserved for special occasions like weddings or festivals and usually has heavy religious overtones. During Ramadan, there is a special emphasis placed on reciting passages from the Koran with music playing in the background. Iranians of all ages are encouraged to take part in these performances.

During the Arab invasion, wrestling was introduced as a form of warfare, and wrestlers would train in the Zur Khaneh (House of Strength), where a special kind of drumming was used to inspire movement. During the nineteenth-century Qajar dynasty, military music became popular, mainly influenced by Iran's relationship with Great Britain. By the twentieth century, a teacher and composer named Ali Naqi khan Vaziri was instrumental in reviving classical forms of Persian music. These compositions were widely heard until the Islamic Revolution, when any music that expressed anything but religious or military themes was banned.

The musicians in this photograph are playing at a teahouse in Kerman, Iran. Current laws in Iran regarding the performing of music are very strict. Women are allowed to publicly perform only in front of female audiences. National television stations in Iran do not show instruments, and if they broadcast music at all, only the musician's face is shown. In 1996, a law was passed that closed music schools and banned music instruction to children under the age of sixteen because of the belief that music corrupts the minds of the youth.

Modern Music

Westernized pop music gained listeners in Iran during the mid-twentieth century with so many of its citizens going abroad for their education. Iranian singers also gained popularity around the same time. One of the most well-known Iranian vocalists is Googoosh, an Iranian woman whose rise to stardom and subsequent silencing by the Islamic government in 1979 continues to fascinate Iranians. Googoosh was a phenomenon of pop culture because she was the first female vocalist who was loved at all levels of Iranian society, gaining acceptance by the rich and adoration from the working classes. The Islamic Revolution put a stop to her career when the government decreed that female vocalists were temptresses. Female vocalists were then forbidden to sing publicly, especially in the presence of men, or even to make recordings.

In fact, under the current regime, music cannot be played publicly at all in Iran, unless it is for religious or military purposes. With the availability of the Internet, many Iranians are now able to listen to music from all over the world. While Western music is strictly outlawed in the country, it can be found on many Web sites and is highly popular.

FAMOUS FOODS AND RECIPES OF IRAN

9

T raditional Persian food, the heart of the Iranian diet, originated thousands of years ago. Because of the region's location on the Silk Road, cities of the empire encountered many different flavors from both Europe and Asia.

Sheep and goats are the main source for meat in Iran since pork is forbidden in the Muslim religion and there is little land for cattle to graze. There are many sheep-herders who roam the countryside with their flocks, taking them to market for selling. Lamb remains the most popular item on the Iranian menu. It is often skewered with vegetables for a *kebob* or stuffed with rice and nuts and then roasted. Around the Caspian Sea, trout and sturgeon are the more popular dishes, while in the villages of nomadic Kurds, chicken is a specialty.

Rice is one of the most important items in an Iranian's daily meal. It is the oldest grain in the world and is very inexpensive to produce. Rice is grown locally, and it can be prepared in a variety of ways making it sweet or spicy. When rice is mixed with another ingredient, like nuts or spices, it becomes *polow*. All kinds of things are mixed into rice to add to its flavor, from sweet berries to fresh herbs. A meat dish is then traditionally served on top of the rice.

The Iranian women in this photograph *(left)* stand in front of a hamburger restaurant in Isfahan. In Iranian cities, fast foods popular in the West such as pizza, fried chicken, hamburgers, and deli sandwiches have become increasingly favored, although hamburgers are often called "sandwiches." Many of these restaurants largely resemble American fast-food chains, but the food varies in quality. This Iranian man *(above)* fishes for endangered sturgeon off the coast of the Caspian Sea. Iran's seafood production has increased over the past year. More than 110 tons of trout and 55 tons of other types of fish were packaged and marketed in the Iranian city of Qom alone.

Borani Esfanaj

This Iranian dish, a common spinach yogurt salad, can be served as an appetizer, a dip, or a side dish.
Serves 6

1 onion, chopped
4 cloves garlic, chopped
1 tablespoon butter
½ teaspoon tumeric
½ teaspoon cayenne pepper (or Tabasco sauce)
½ teaspoon curry powder
1 teaspoon cumin
¼ teaspoon cinnamon
1 package chopped spinach
1 cup plain yogurt

Sauté onion and garlic in butter until soft. Add the spices and cook for a few minutes. Mix in the spinach and yogurt. Salt to taste.
Nush-e jan! (Enjoy this food of life!)

Breads in Iran come in all different shapes and sizes. On the streets of Iran, there are always bread shops that have either a simple griddle or a stone oven to cook *naan*, a flat bread, or *sang-gak*, which is slightly puffy. There are many foods that can be easily eaten by hand or scooped up with bread, like stuffed vegetables called *dolmeh* or *koftas*, which are spicy meatballs that are made of lamb.

The fruits of Iran are well-known for their flavors and varieties since the climate and soil of the country is well suited to its growth. Melons are particularly popular because they grow extremely well in the Iranian deserts. They were discovered by travelers in the time of Marco Polo and are still sought after by tourists. Melons are very popular for dessert, as are pomegranates, quinces, pears, grapes, dates, apricots, and peaches. Sometimes fruit is sweetened with rose water or crushed and frozen into sherbet.

In the city of Shiraz, a rose-flavored ice drink called *palouden* made with a variety of fruits is served. Yogurt mixed with water and mint is also a very

popular beverage. Tea, known in Iran as *chai*, is the national beverage and is grown on mountain slopes and around the Caspian region. Alcohol is forbidden by Islamic law.

Distant Influences

Persians borrowed freely from other cultures to establish their own distinct cuisine. The kabob was from Turkey; vegetables and meats wrapped in grape leaves from Greece; dishes with figs, dates, and lambs from Arabia; and curries from India. These taste sensations merged and mingled as traders traveled throughout the region or invading armies captured new territory. When the Arabs moved into India, they introduced rice dishes. Today offerings like *kurmah*, *kofta*, *briani*, and *pilaus* are all well-known dishes featuring rice with meats and sauces.

Squatting on the floor of her home, this Iranian woman makes *breaval* cake. In many households, Iranians prefer to eat at low tables on the floor. Cutlery includes a spoon and a fork, and Iranians consider it inappropriate to eat with the left hand. The modern Iranian diet normally consists of rice, bread, vegetables, and fruit. Meat, used to add flavor to the meal, is rarely its dominant ingredient. Fresh herbs and spices, especially saffron, nutmeg, and cardamom, are used in many Iranian recipes.

Much of the food grown or gathered in Iran is exported to other countries. The pistachios that grow on the mountainsides near Rafsanjan are the third

---

Snack Foods

Iranian markets sell all kinds of traditional snack foods, including the following.

Lavashak – plum pulp spread into thin layers and dried into sheets
Laboo – baked beets
Chaghale badooom – unripe almonds
Goje sabz – sour green plums
Fresh pistachios and other nuts along with dried fruits and popped corn are also commonly sold by street vendors.

---

largest export in Iran. The roe (eggs) of the sturgeon fish, also known as caviar, is a great exported delicacy often too expensive for the average Iranian citizen.

Chai Customs

The Russians introduced tea drinking to Iranian society in the nineteenth century. Prior to that, most Iranians drank coffee. These days, tea has firmly replaced coffee as Iran's national drink. Relaxing over a glass of chai is a daily custom. A samovar, which is an urn often made of copper, is always on the fire filled with hot chai. Even people going on picnics will take a portable samovar with them. The chai is usually very strong and served in a small glass. Lumps of sugar, which don't go into the glass but instead sit on the tongue or are held between the teeth, often accompany each serving.

Western Influences

Iranians remain very traditional about their food, although before 1979, Western influences were felt with the arrival of processed foods. McDonald's® could be found in downtown Tehran, and Coca-Cola® was bottled in Iran starting in 1956. Since 1995, when then president Bill Clinton prohibited U.S. companies from doing business with Iran, Coca-Cola cannot be found. But you can find certain soda factories reusing old Coca-Cola bottles by filling them with their own version of cola. While some Iranian stores try to get around the embargo by importing soft drinks from other countries, such as Saudi Arabia, American soda is normally hard to find. Iranian companies have developed their own colas such as Zam Zam and Parsi Cola.

Halal and Haram

Halal is an Arabic word that means lawful or permitted. The opposite of halal is *haram*. While these terms apply to all facets of Islamic life, they are especially important when used regarding food. If something is not clearly halal or haram, it is considered *mashbooh*, which means questionable. The following products are halal, or acceptable: milk (from cows, sheep, camels, and goats), honey, fish, plants that are not intoxicants, fresh or naturally frozen vegetables, fresh or dried fruits, and nuts, grains, and legumes.

Haram foods are not acceptable: swine and pork by-products, animals that are slaughtered in an improper manner, alcohol and intoxicants, carnivorous animals, birds of prey, and land animals without external ears.

These Iranian men sell goods at a bazaar. Iranian bread is of high quality, is often inexpensive, and can be found anywhere in the country. The standard Iranian breakfast consists of bread with feta cheese, jam, honey, or butter. Most people think that the best-tasting Iranian bread is called *sangak*, which is a thick oval-shaped loaf that is baked on a bed of stones. This bread is so popular and in demand that there is a black market for sangak with people willing to pay more than the normal price to obtain it.

DAILY LIFE AND CUSTOMS IN IRAN

verage Iranians typically rise very early in the morning, sharing with one another a common early-to-rise mentality that has much to do with the weather.

An Iranian workday normally occurs over an eight-hour period, with factories and schools opening during the early morning hours. Each day begins with a simple breakfast of chai and bread. Fresh bread and cheese can normally be purchased at various shops or street vendors. When the heat is intense during the middle of the day, Iranians often break for lunch, which is normally their largest meal. Some

will go home and see their families during this break, or rest and then return to work later in the evening. Another much shorter break is always taken in the midafternoon for chai, and a lighter dinner takes place around 9 PM. Most shops remain open late to accommodate people's schedule.

Iranian Muslims must also stop working in order to pray. There are five calls to prayer throughout each day—at dawn, early afternoon, midafternoon, early evening, and at night. All Muslims must stop to pray when they hear the call of the muezzin. Friday is the Muslim holy day of observation, so all businesses and schools close on Thursday afternoon and remain closed throughout the day on Friday.

A motorcyclist (left) carries mattresses. Iran's location on international trade routes between northern, southern, eastern, and western points in the Middle East provides the country with a demand for international transport services. Iran is easily accessible to Turkmenistan, Afghanistan, Azerbaijan, Armenia, Pakistan, Iraq, and Turkey, as well as ports on the Persian Gulf, Gulf of Oman, and the Caspian Sea, through a network of highways. Two farmers (above) load a mule. On many Iranian farms, mules are used for heavy labor such as riding and transporting goods and farm equipment.

At one time, Iranian handicrafts such as embroidered items were viewed as objects that had an artistic value. Today, they are an integral part of the country's overall economy. More than one million Iranians are employed to create hundreds of different handicrafts, just like the woman embroidering in this photograph. Each year, more than 20,000 apprentices attend various craft training classes.

In the countryside, life changes are more seasonal and revolve around the tasks and work of running a farm. Before 1960, much of Iran's farmlands were owned by wealthy landowners, who then rented them for high prices and kept most of the profits from crops. The last shah, Mohammed Reza, began a program of redistribution of land back to Iranian farmers. After the 1979 revolution, Islamic authorities continued this redistribution of land. They helped reestablish villages that had previously been without water and electricity. Today, under the guidance of the Crusade for Construction, most villages have paved roads, telephone lines, electricity, and irrigation pumps. These villages are usually organized around a central square and mosque where people gather to worship.

Family Traditions

Since 1979, the average size of a family in Iran has decreased. Prior to the revolution,

This metalsmith works in Shiraz, Iran. Working with metal has been an art form and economic activity in Iran since ancient times. In Iran, metal is used for ornamental, domestic, and practical purposes. Gold and silver were metals utilized by the wealthy elite of ancient Persia. The most common modern items made of metal are tea sets, bowls, trays, vases, and jewelry.

This Iranian woman is weaving a small Persian carpet. The quality of Persian rugs is not only determined by the material used, such as wool or silk yarns, but also by the amount of knots. A low-grade carpet has thirty to fifty knots per square inch, while a higher quality one has up to one hundred. Museum-quality rugs have five hundred or more knots per square inch.

married couples were encouraged to raise large families with six or more children. Today, fewer families are as large. No longer encouraged to have as many children since Iran's economy and health care system are less stable, the role of Iranian women is changing. The average size of an Iranian family has decreased by half. Although typical incomes have also dropped, the country is not impoverished. Actually, Iran has a higher standard of living than many neighboring countries such as Pakistan, Afghanistan, and India.

Caring for the elderly is traditionally kept in the family. Since seniors are highly respected and considered wise, this is a natural and welcomed choice for most families. While Iran's average life expectancy is lower than that in many Westernized countries, it has risen recently with most Iranians now living into their seventies. This is partly because the Constitution of 1979 instituted government coverage for the care of older Iranians along with benefits for others who are ill or disabled.

Inside the home, there are often divisions of space based on gender. There may be places in the house where only women can be present and other spaces reserved only for men. The customs of divorce are also more liberal. Under Islamic law, the man merely has to repeat "I divorce you" three times in front of his wife to make a divorce official. He must then give her whatever is promised under the *marh*, or marriage contract.

Social Life

Iranian entertainment largely revolves around the home, where eating, talking, and socializing are favorite activities. Since alcohol is banned, a samovar is always on the fire for chai, which is drunk as a custom. Although television and radio are also very popular, all programs are censored by the government to remove graphic violence, sex, or any behavior that would be considered uncharacteristic for a devout Muslim.

In rural Iran, storytelling and visits to the mosque are frequent leisure activities. Sometimes, traveling actors, musicians, poets, or puppeteers will perform in the village square. People may also retire to an underground bathhouse, usually built near the source of a hot water spring, for relaxation. In the city, many men enter teahouses (once called *kafekhanna*, or coffeehouse) where they will talk, socialize, and play chess. Although the game was invented in India in 400 BC, Iranians started playing chess around the same time. They used the word "shah" for king and from this comes the word "chess." "Checkmate" comes from an ancient Persian word *shahmat*, which means "the king is helpless."

A large social scene among young people has developed with the availability of the Internet. Visiting chat rooms and Web sites offers a freedom of expression and opportunity previously banned to teenagers in Iran. According to the Iranian government, 400,000 people went online in 2001, and that number continues to rise steadily. Many Iranian Web sites are registered in other countries to prevent the government from shutting them down.

The Island of Kish

In 1989, Kish, a tiny coral island off the coast of Iran in the Persian Gulf, became a holiday destination when the government loosened many of the restrictions that citizens are subject to on the mainland. They did this in order to keep Iranian citizens from spending their vacation money in places like Turkey or Saudi Arabia. Although the beaches are segregated, men and women can rent speedboats to ride on together. They can also sit, talk, and even legally hold hands in public. Women are expected to look modest, but they don't have to wear the usually long, loose coats and headscarves. And although music for social pleasure is banned in Iran, it is permitted in Kish. Tourists can hear everything from Western-styled music to traditional Persian songs. There are many shopping malls, and all items are duty-free, meaning that taxes are not due when Iranians return home with goods. Occasionally, however, Iran's Islamic hard-liners will make their criticisms known, as they did when they shut down a theater showing a Western film. Friday is still observed as a holy day with closed shops and restaurants, but Kish mostly operates free of the strict rules imposed on the mainland.

Recreation

Competitive sports became popular in Iran during the early twentieth century, when Christian missionaries introduced tennis, basketball, and swimming into the country.

Primarily a male endeavor, soccer became especially popular and is still played today. Wrestling, horse racing, and weight lifting are also very popular. In Iran's larger cities, urban Iranians enjoy squash in air-conditioned courts, which are plentiful.

In rural areas, the sports of camel racing and hunting are enjoyed, while some Iranians still train falcons, eagles, or hawks for sport. Falconry, where a trained bird dives down on prey like mice and other rodents and is then retrieved by the falconer, or master, was the sport of the Persian nobility. It is no longer as popular today.

Wrestling continues to be an age-old sport that is practiced at the Zur Khaneh. This pastime originated as a form of warfare during the Arab invasion of Persia. It was a secret society where members were sworn to do everything they could to drive out invading forces. The members would be given vigorous training. As in the ancient tradition, live drumming and the chanting of verses normally accompanies wrestling today.

These young Iranian boys pose with a soccer ball. Soccer is the country's most popular sport, and games are held throughout the country, often on Friday evenings. Tehran has ten soccer stadiums, one of which seats up to 100,000 fans. While Iranian boys play during the summer months in neighborhood competitions, girls are forced to play sports in enclosed areas away from members of the opposite sex. As adults, many men play professionally in soccer leagues, on Iran's World Cup soccer team, or as part of European teams. Iranian women may also compete in sports, but mostly do so in the areas of shooting, fencing, and archery.

EDUCATION AND WORK IN IRAN

E ducation for males has been a high priority in Iran since the early centuries of Islam, when Persia was considered a great center of culture. At that time, higher education was limited only to the wealthy, or to Muslims who were devoting their lives to Islam.

Systematic education did not become a reality until the time of Reza Shah Pahlavi in the mid-1940s. During this time, regular primary school became a requirement for all children through the fifth grade. Young girls and women were also given the opportunity to attend classes at primary schools and colleges. The shah raised the standards even further in the 1960s by opening more universities and teacher-training schools in order to educate a growing populace. Most Iranians needed to gain literacy skills. The government sent out 35,000 teachers under what was called Literacy Corps into the cities and countryside to teach people how to read and write. Education in Iran is free. More than 70 percent of Iran's total population is literate.

A teacher lectures to a group of students (*left*) in a secretly run school in Iran. Although this classroom has both male and female students, Iranian schools by law are non-secular and are segregated by gender. Since the revolution of 1979, the Shiite government has mandated that children receive daily religious education. In the classroom, teachers largely direct lessons without encouraging an open dialogue between students. This elderly teacher from a small village (*above*) gives a girl a reading lesson. The Iranian government provides free compulsory education for children between the ages of six and ten. In rural areas such as this, many children lack the facilities of a modern school and are usually taught in two half-day shifts.

The girls in this photograph are studying in a cooperative Islamic school in Tehran, which is funded through government subsidies, donations, and tuition payments. Starting in the earliest grades, Iranian students are assigned a lot of memorization and written homework. Upon entering high school, students choose a specialized path of study, such as one devoted to academics, only math and science, or vocational and technical training. For example, if a student chooses math and science, then he or she does not have to take any writing or literature classes. Academic, math, and science directives prepare students for university study, which is free for students who pass the national entrance exam.

(Comparatively, 97 percent of the population in the United States is literate.)

By 1979, Iran had sixteen universities, including the large University of Tehran, which dates back to 1934. After the revolution, the Revolutionary Council temporarily closed these schools. Under the supervision of the Ministry of Education and Training, schools began reopening with each one overseen by a ruling mullah. Although many teachers left the country during the post-revolutionary upheaval, newer educational training institutes have recently become established.

Women have had more educational opportunities after the revolution, although all places of learning continue to separate girls from boys and women from men. Iranian women are among the most educated and accomplished in the Muslim world. They comprise half of all new admissions into universities compared with one-third of university

enrollment during the 1970s. Today, approximately one in three Iranian physicians is female. In a country where women's rights are so tightly controlled, the availability of higher education is something of which women can take advantage.

There is quite a difference between education in Iran's cities versus its rural areas. Primary school is required by the government for all children from the age of six until twelve. Not all families abide by these rules, however, either because schools are too far away or because they need the child to work in the family business or farm. In some rural areas, daughters will attend primary school and then remain at home with the family under their parents' guidance while the sons continue their education. Secondary school continues to the age of eighteen and is not required by law. It is very strict, and the students must pass a qualifying exam to be admitted.

The Iranian government is introducing technology in the classroom, as shown in this photograph of young girls learning how to use the computer. Computer literacy for the population is a major goal of the government, which is currently focused on providing Internet access to primary school students so that these children will be the next generation of technologically capable adults. Efforts are also being made to integrate technology into institutions of higher education so college students will be less eager to study abroad.

At the end of every year there are exams. If a student fails even one subject, he or she will have to repeat the entire year. The September-June school year begins each week on a Saturday morning and finishes on Thursdays at noon.

Sex Education

Because of the strict rules of the Islamic Republic of Iran against relations between unmarried men and women, any talk of sex education in Iran is virtually forbidden. This presents a challenge to the Iranian Center for Disease Control as it combats a rising number of cases of AIDS and other sexually transmitted diseases. A pamphlet distributed by that organization writes, "Trust in God in order to resist Satanic temptations," as a way to steer young people away from practicing sex outside of marriage. It makes no mention of any form of preventative contraceptive. Although condoms are available in pharmacies, the government's point of view is that telling teenagers about them will be seen as an encouragement to have sex.

Many in Iran feel that the best way to educate young people and deal with this problem is to use the traditions of the Islamic religion. There are some clerics and members of parliament who suggest the practice of "temporary marriage," which is when a man and woman draw up a contract of marriage for a brief period of time. Some feel that by enacting this temporary marriage the taboo would be broken and couples could then receive contraceptives from health authorities just as married men and women do.

These students in a class for Kashgai and Mamesani boys at the Shiraz Tribal High School are dressed in traditional attire. This school was stared in 1967 and encourages a curriculum and atmosphere for the once nomadic tribes to continue their tribal culture. According to Iran's Cultural Constitution, ratified in 1911, primary education for all children, whether living in urban, rural, or tribal areas, is compulsory.

The first car made in Iran was called the Paykan and was manufactured in 1967 by a British company. Iranians are more willing to buy foreign cars because of their overall quality and lower prices, a trend that is causing the Iranian motor vehicle industry to suffer. In response, Iran's Ministry of Industry has now mandated stricter codes and inspection regulations on outgoing vehicles to improve their quality, an effort that is expected to boost the country's economy. Presently in Iran there is about one car per twenty-two people.

Children are normally granted a two-week break in March for the New Year. Students are required to attend classes during the month of Ramadan.

Youth Culture

The majority of today's Iranians were born after the 1979 revolution and have never lived under anything but an Islamic Republic. However, outside influences such as the Internet have increased substantially in the last decade, exposing Iranian youth to different aspects of liberal lifestyles. Many schools have computers in the classrooms, which are closely monitored by teachers and clerics. Some of this technology allows them to interact with students in other countries. While the Iranian government tries to control its citizens' access to outside information, the Internet has invited a new world into the lives of many Iranians.

Internet sites reveal deep-seated curiosity about taboo subjects regarding the opposite sex. Many chat rooms have become forums for exploring topics that cannot be discussed in regular society. While girls and boys may flirt in cyberspace, they still maintain a distance from each other on Iran's streets.

The Workforce

Before the 1979 revolution, many Iranians left the country for educational opportunities and returned with a variety of customs and business practices. These days, Iran is self-sufficient, keeping its workforce inside the country with goods like oil, caviar, and pistachio nuts being exported. During the time of the shahs, many Iranians relocated to major cities from outlying villages. Today, because of government improvements in local services, many people remain in their hometowns. It now makes economic sense for people to stay in their villages

The man in this photograph is selling fruit from the back of a donkey. For thousands of years, farmers have irrigated their land on the central plateau by using *qanats*, which are underground water channels. About one-third of all Iranians work as farmers, sustaining crops such as wheat, barley, rice, cotton, sugarcane, fruits, vegetables, and nuts. Agriculture is Iran's largest export after oil and handmade carpets, and Iranian pistachio nuts are regarded as the best in the world. It is the goal of the Iranian government to become a self-sufficient nation regarding food production.

Mud bricks, like the ones made by this Iranian man in the town of Ardekan, are the world's oldest building material. Even today houses and buildings in Iran are sometimes made out of mud bricks, which are a combination of water and mud that is reinforced with hay and then dried in the sun. Mud bricks are very energy efficient, and structures built from them are commonly warm in the winter and cool in the summer.

because the government's Crusade for Construction plan has paved thousands of miles of road, built bridges, installed irrigation systems, and increased electrical availability. Now almost 90 percent of Iran's outlying villages can function in a modern way and compete in the business marketplace.

A majority of Iranians work in the oil and mining industries. The government also encourages the growth of companies that make paper, aircraft parts, shoes, and pharmaceuticals so that Iran will be less dependent on outside countries for imports. Farmers make up a high percentage of the workforce tending to crops such as wheat, barley, rice, sugar, cotton, raisins, dates, tea, and tobacco. Almonds and pistachios are also a great source of export revenue for Iran.

Iran's fishing industry on the Caspian coast is more prosperous than on the Persian Gulf. This is a result of damage sustained in the 1980s during the Iraq-Iran War. Today, Iranian fishermen catch huge amounts of sturgeon whose eggs are then exported as caviar.

Islamic law recognizes that men and women are not identical but rather are complementary to each other's needs. Shiite Islam has a strong history of female role models such as Fatima, daughter of Muhammad, and Zayhab, granddaughter of Muhammad. There are also many female Islamic preachers and religious leaders in Iran that encourage Iranian women to participate in religious activities. Many women also work in education and other professions. In 1998, more women entered Iran's universities than men.

Iranian men and women often hold more than one job to make ends meet. Inflation was driven higher in 1979 when foreign investments and trade relations with numerous countries declined or were halted. Iran's economy also suffered from the long war with Iraq, which strained much of its workforce, removing men from their jobs to fight in a war. The conflict also affected oil production when many wells situated between the two countries in the Persian Gulf were damaged. Throughout this period and into the 1990s, trade embargoes set by the United States combined with a doubling of the population sent the country into an economic tumble. Despite those conditions, the average living standard in Iran is higher than those in many neighboring countries. Iran's strong religious authority appears to keep its citizens close-knit, while the younger generation seems to be successfully integrating its strong Islamic beliefs within the larger modern world.

IRAN
AT A GLANCE

HISTORY

The Persian civilization is one of the oldest in the world. Archaeologists have found evidence that people lived in the region as far back as 100,000 years before Jesus Christ. At least 10,000 years ago, the area had a civilization that farmed, raised animals, and made pottery. Some of the world's earliest cities in southwestern Persia were thriving by 6000 BC. Its people were known as the Elamites. They were ruled by a king and had an organized priesthood. The religion of the time was known as Zoroastrianism. The Elamites traveled over the Zagros Mountains and began to take over more land.

The word "Iran" comes from "Aryan," which means "noble," and was the name of the tribes that spilled into the region from central Asia beginning about 1500 BC. They were known as the Medes, Persians, Parthians, and Bactrians, and are all ancestors of modern Iranians. In 553 BC, Cyrus the Great, leader of the Achaemenid clan, invaded the Medes territory in the north and east and established an empire. In 334 BC, Alexander the Great conquered the region. For hundreds of years, the Greeks and Romans fought over Persia until the Sassanid dynasty came into power in 224 BC and the region was once again ruled by Persians. This was an incredibly rich period for art and literature. It was also the first example of a developing class system with priests, warriors, scribes, and commoners all establishing rights in the towns. When the Arabs invaded in the early seventh century AD, they brought with them the teachings of Muhammad and Islam. Persians then became Muslims.

Throughout the thirteenth and fourteenth centuries, different tribes came through Persia and conquered the region, including the greatly feared Genghis Khan and his Mongol hordes. The Persians were able to regain control in the sixteenth century, and Shah Abbas established the city of Isfahan. European influences grew stronger, and during the late eighteenth century, Iran was under the rule of the Qajars. British and Russian involvement in the country became unbearable until a military officer named Reza Khan seized power with British support and brought down the Qajar dynasty. He declared himself the shah (ruler), and in 1935, he officially changed the country's name from Persia to Iran. The pressures of foreign relations during World War II forced him to abdicate and pass the role to his son, Mohammed Reza Shah Pahlavi, the last reigning shah of Iran.

The years following the war were very prosperous for Iran and saw many changes in the country. What was known as the White Revolution in the 1960s ushered in a time of freedom for women, growth of the economy, and freedom of speech. Many of the traditional Islamic clerics were unhappy with these reforms. The shah also became increasingly controlling and outlawed all political parties but his own. In 1979, after mounting pressure on his government, the shah fled the country and Ruhollah Khomeini returned from his exile in France to become the ayatollah, or supreme leader. Under his rule, Iran became an Islamic republic and returned to strict Islamic beliefs. Relations with the United States became especially strained when sixty-six people were taken hostage from the United States Embassy in demand for the shah's return from the United States, where he was receiving medical treatment. The hostage crisis lasted for 444 days. The shah died in Egypt in 1980, and Iran became involved in border conflicts with Iraq, which lasted throughout the 1980s. Today Iran is ruled by the Ayatollah Seyed Ali Khamenei, a respected Islamic cleric who took over after Khomeini died of a heart attack in 1989. Iran's president is Mohammad Khatami, who was elected in 1997 and is now serving his second and final term.

Economy

The Iranian government controls 95 percent of the economy, which means that there is very little business that is conducted without government involvement. Although President Khatami promised to bring about reforms that would allow citizens to be involved in private businesses, this goal has been difficult because Iran is ruled by religious clerics whose focus is not economic policy. Also, the office of president in Iran has little power to push through laws since that is the job of the ayatollah.

Unemployment in Iran is relatively high, although the revenues from oil production, the country's number one export, subsidize food and housing for the poor and gasoline for the middle class. The annual average income for

Iranians in U.S. dollars was $2,320, according to 1999 statistics. The economy grew worse after the Islamic Republic took over in 1979 when many of the country's businessmen, technical workers, and companies left the country. Also, the war with Iraq and trade sanctions by the United States, combined with a growing population, put a strain on Iran's economic health.

Inflation in 2000 rose by about 16 percent, meaning that everything was more expensive than it had been the year before. Since the Iranian economy depends on its ability to sell oil, worldwide prices are very important. In 2000, oil prices rose substantially and have remained fairly high, bringing money steadily into the country. Other exports like Persian carpets, caviar, and pistachio nuts also help the economy. Overall, Iran's economy is a mixture of state-owned oil, village agriculture, and small-scale private trading and service ventures. The government discourages foreign investments and relations. In 1997, when President Khatami was elected, relations with European countries became stronger. Even tensions with America eased a bit, although recently, with world tensions increasing higher as terrorism becomes a consistent threat, feelings between the East and the West are again strained. In 2002, U.S. president George W. Bush named Iran as part of an evil axis along with North Korea and Iraq because of its alleged threat to U.S. national security. This pronouncement has once again put Iran at odds with the United States.

Government and Politics

In 1979, when Iran became an Islamic republic, the religious cleric Ruhollah Khomeini and his supporters wrote a constitution to govern its citizens. Iran became a theocratic republic, which means the country is ruled by a divine authority, or ayatollah. This position is non-elected and held by the leader for life. After Khomeini's death in 1989, the Ayatollah Seyed Ali Khamenei became supreme leader. The constitution recognizes this supreme leader as the chief of state. He has the ultimate authority over the government, commands the armed forces, and approves all candidates for office. He is assisted by the Council of Guardians, which consists of six religious leaders and six lawyers. These guardians look over all the laws, court decisions, and government actions to make sure they meet the principles of Shiite Islam.

There are elections every four years to select a president who becomes the head of government. This position holds little power. The president is largely a figurehead, although he can influence government decisions. Mohammad Khatami was elected in 1997, replacing Ali Akbar Hashemi Rafsanjani. Khatami was re-elected in 2001. Khatami is known as a reformist president, meaning he has spoken of softening some hard-line Islamic laws. He has also tried to allow Iranian citizens more personal freedoms. While this movement has been marginally successful, there are still security forces assigned by the Iranian government that patrol the streets seeking to combat "moral corruption."

Since 2001, there has been an appointed vice president, Dr. Mohammad Reza Aref-Yazdi. There is also a council of ministers that oversees day-to-day administration of various branches of the government, such as labor, economic planning, social welfare, and commerce. Iran's legislature is called Majlis, sometimes referred to as its parliament. It consists of 290 seats filled by elected officials who make the country's laws under the supervision of the Council of Guardians.

Iran is split into twenty-eight provinces called *ostanha* (the plural of *ostan*). Local governors are appointed by the government to work with religious officials known as *anjumans* to ensure that citizens are abiding by Islamic laws. Appointed *mullahs* have the freedom to enter homes and businesses to check for violations of these laws. According to the constitution, Iran's justice system is based on *sharia* (or *shari'ah*), which is traditional Islamic law. The supreme court meets in Iran's capital of Tehran, and there are a series of lower courts throughout the country. The High Council of the Judiciary consists of four *mujtahids* (experts in Islamic law). In 1983, the penal code was rewritten to include traditional punishments called *qisas*, or "retributions." These punishments, for crimes like theft or adultery, range from flogging and stoning to the amputation of a limb.

Iranian men must serve in the military for two years. Iran has strengthened diplomatic relationships with other Middle Eastern and south Asian countries like Afghanistan, Pakistan, and Saudi Arabia, but retains an antagonistic relationship with neighboring Iraq, with which the country fought a border war for the better part of the 1980s. Although former U.S. president Bill Clinton worked on strengthening ties with Iran during the 1990s, current president George W. Bush has not. Iran does have export and import relationships with Japan, Italy, South Korea, France, and China.

TIMELINE

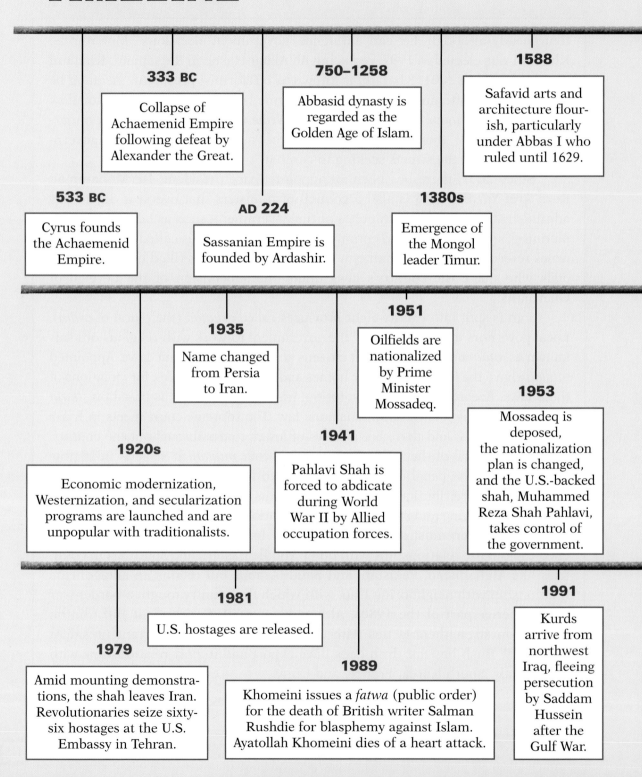

333 BC
Collapse of Achaemenid Empire following defeat by Alexander the Great.

750–1258
Abbasid dynasty is regarded as the Golden Age of Islam.

1588
Safavid arts and architecture flourish, particularly under Abbas I who ruled until 1629.

533 BC
Cyrus founds the Achaemenid Empire.

AD 224
Sassanian Empire is founded by Ardashir.

1380s
Emergence of the Mongol leader Timur.

1951
Oilfields are nationalized by Prime Minister Mossadeq.

1935
Name changed from Persia to Iran.

1953
Mossadeq is deposed, the nationalization plan is changed, and the U.S.-backed shah, Muhammed Reza Shah Pahlavi, takes control of the government.

1941
Pahlavi Shah is forced to abdicate during World War II by Allied occupation forces.

1920s
Economic modernization, Westernization, and secularization programs are launched and are unpopular with traditionalists.

1981
U.S. hostages are released.

1991
Kurds arrive from northwest Iraq, fleeing persecution by Saddam Hussein after the Gulf War.

1979
Amid mounting demonstrations, the shah leaves Iran. Revolutionaries seize sixty-six hostages at the U.S. Embassy in Tehran.

1989
Khomeini issues a *fatwa* (public order) for the death of British writer Salman Rushdie for blasphemy against Islam. Ayatollah Khomeini dies of a heart attack.

1736

Safavids are deposed by Nadir Shah Afshar, who ruled until 1747.

1801–1828

Britain exercises influence and fights Iran in 1856–1857 over claims to Herat (Afghanistan).

1925

Qajar dynasty is overthrown, with some British help, in a coup by Col. Reza Khan, a nationalist later crowned shah with the title Reza Shah Pahlavi.

1790

Rise of the Qajars.

1963

Protesters, who demand the release of the arrested fundamentalist Shiite Muslim leader Khomeini, are killed by troops.

1977

The death in An Najaf of Mustafa, eldest son of the exiled Ayatollah Ruhollah Khomeini, sparks demonstrations.

1978

Opposition to the shah is organized from France by traditionalist Ayatollah Ruhollah Khomeini.

1970s

World oil prices bring rapid economic expansion.

1995

President Clinton prohibits U.S. companies from doing business with Iran.

2000

Ali Akbar Mohtashami, a former radical, is elected to lead the reforming majority in Iran's parliament.

2002

President Bush declares Iran part of an "evil axis," brought about by terrorist events in America on September 11, 2001.

1997

Reformist politician Seyyed Muhammad Khatami is elected president.

2001

Khatami is re-elected.

IRAN

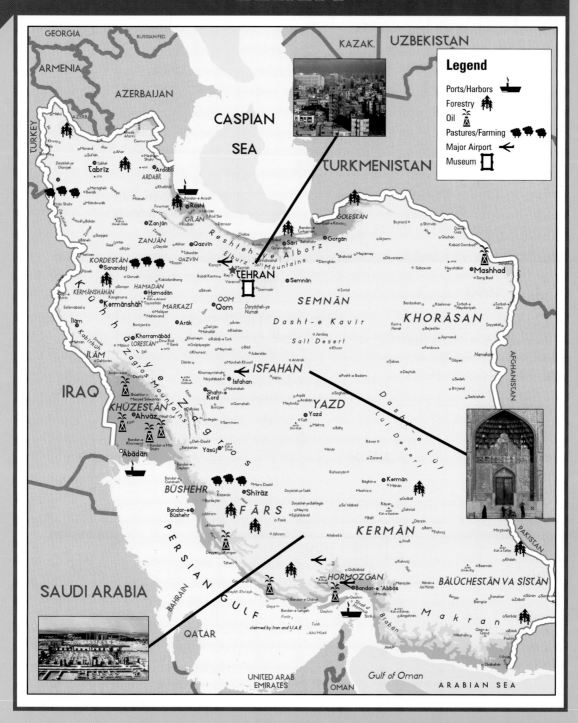

Legend
- Ports/Harbors
- Forestry
- Oil
- Pastures/Farming
- Major Airport
- Museum

ECONOMIC FACT SHEET

GDP in US$: $413 billion

GDP Sectors: Services 48%, agriculture 24%, industry 28%

Land Use: Arable land 10%, permanent crops 1%, permanent pastures 27%, forests and woodland 7%, agriculture 11.1%

Currency: 1 U.S. Dollar = 1,741.25 Iranian Rial (2002)

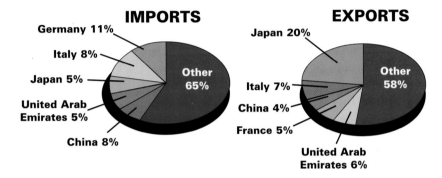

IMPORTS

Germany 11%
Italy 8%
Japan 5%
United Arab Emirates 5%
China 8%
Other 65%

EXPORTS

Japan 20%
Italy 7%
China 4%
France 5%
United Arab Emirates 6%
Other 58%

Workforce: Agriculture 33%, Industry 25%, Services 42%

Major Agricultural Products: Wheat, rice, sugar beets, fruits, nuts, cotton, dairy products, wool, caviar

Major Exports: $24.6 billion. Petroleum, carpets, fruits and nuts, iron and steel, chemicals

Major Imports: $19.6 billion. Industrial raw materials, foodstuffs and other consumer goods, technical services, military supplies

Significant Trading Partners:

Export: Japan, Italy, United Arab Emirates, South Korea, France, China

Import: Germany, South Korea, Italy, United Arab Emirates, France, Japan

Rate of Unemployment: 14%

Highways: Total 87,116 miles (140,200 km), paved 30,720 miles (49,440 km), unpaved 56,395 miles (90,760 km)

Railroads: 3,809 miles (6,130 km)

Waterways: 56,395 miles (904 km)

Airports: Total 337

POLITICAL FACT SHEET

Official Country Name: Islamic Republic of Iran (formerly Persia)

Official Flag: Three equal horizontal bands of green, white, and red. The national emblem (a stylized representation of the word "Allah") in red is centered in the white band. *"Allah Akbar"* (God Is Great) in white Arabic script is repeated eleven times along the bottom edge of the green band and eleven times along the top edge of the red band.

System of Government: Theocratic republic

National Anthem:

"Ey Iran" (Adopted in 1990)
Author unknown, but music composed by Hassan Riahi

Upwards on the horizon rises the Eastern Sun,
The sight of the true Religion.
Bahman—the brilliance of our Faith.
Your message, O Imam, of independence and freedom
is imprinted on our souls.
O Martyrs! The time of your cries of pain rings in our ears.
Enduring, continuing, eternal,
The Islamic Republic of Iran.

Federal Structure: Chief of state: supreme leader, the ayatollah. Head of government: the president, vice president. Cabinet: Council of Ministers selected by the president, Legislative Branch: Islamic Consultative Assembly or Majlis

Number of Registered Voters: 38,700,000 (2000)

CULTURAL FACT SHEET

Official Languages: Persian and Persian dialect (Farsi) 58%, Turkic and Turkic dialect 26%, Kurdish 9%, Luri 2%, Balochi 1%, Arabic 1%, Turkish 1%, other 2%

Major Religions: Shiite Muslim 89%; Sunni Muslim 10%; Sufi, Zoroastrian, Jewish, Christian and Baha'i 1%

Capital: Tehran

Population: 66,128,965

Ethnic Groups: Persian 51%, Axeri 24%, Gilaki and Mazandarani 8%, Kurd 7%, Arab 3%, Lur 2%, Baloch 2%, Turkmen 2%, other 1%

Life Expectancy: Males 68.61 years, females 71.37 years

Time: Greenwich Mean Time plus three and one half hours

Literacy Rate: 72.1%

National Flower: Red tulip

Cultural Leaders:
  Fine Arts: Kamran Abbasi, Ehsan Afshar, Pantea Rahmani, Katayoun Moghadam, Bhid Nasirian, Freydoon Rasouli
  Literature: Tannaz Ebadollahi, Setareh Sabety, Monir Taha, Sheema Kalbasi, Leila Farjami, Solmaz Sharif
  Entertainment: Bahram Beyzaie (director), Majid Majidi (writer/director) Masoud Raouf (director), Shahrbanoo (director), Parviz Sayyad (director/ actor), Googoosh, Shahram Nazeri, Seyed Ali Khan, Ardavan Kamkar, Dariush Saghafi, Hassan Rangraz (wrestler)

National Holidays and Festivals

February 11 (Islamic Revolution Day)	April 5 (Anniversary of 1963 Uprising)
March 20 (Nationalization of Iranian Oil Industry)	June 4 (Death of Ayatollah Khomeini)
March 21–24 Now Ruz (New Year)	June 5 Anniversary of Uprising Against the Shah
April 1 (Islamic Republic Day)	

Working Life:
  Workweek: Saturday—Thursday noon (Friday off for day of prayer)
  Workday: average eight-hour days—40 hours per week

GLOSSARY

abdicate (AB-dih-kayt) To give up power from a throne or high office.

archaeologist (ar-kee-AH-luh-jist) A person who studies the remains of people and cultures through fossils, relics, and artifacts.

arid (AH-rid) Excessively dry.

ayatollah (AH-yah-toh-lah) Title given to pious and learned religious men at the top of the Islamic Shiite hierarchy.

Buddhism (BOO-dih-zum) A religion of eastern and central Asia that grew out of the teachings of Gautama Buddha, whose main idea is that suffering is inherent in life.

caravan (KAR-uh-van) A company of travelers on a journey.

Christianity (kris-chee-A-nih-tee) The religion derived from Jesus Christ, based on the Bible as sacred scripture.

coup (KOO) A french term meaning "blow to the state" that refers to a sudden, unexpected overthrow of government.

democratic (deh-muh-KRA-tik) Relating to or available to the broad masses of the people.

devout (dih-VOWT) Devoted to religion or to religious duties or exercises.

dynasty (DY-nas-tee) A succession of rulers of the same line of descent.

fundamentalism (fun-DUH-ment-al-izm) A movement or attitude stressing strict and literal adherence to principles.

hereditary (huh-REH-dih-teh-ree) Having title or possession through inheritance by birth.

imperialism (ihm-PEER-ee-uhl-ih-zum) The policy of extending power and dominion of a nation, especially by territorial acquisition.

impoverished (im-POV-urh-ished) To deprive of strength, richness, or fertility by depleting or draining of something essential.

inflation (in-FLAY-shun) An increase in the volume of money and credit relative to available goods and services resulting in a continuing rise in the general price level.

Judaism (JOO-dee-ih-zum) A religion developed among the ancient Hebrews and characterized by belief in one transcendent god who has revealed himself to Abraham, Moses, and the Hebrew prophets.

massacre (MA-sih-ker) The act of killing a number of helpless or unresisting people.

migrate (MY-grayt) To move from one place to another.

monarchy (MAH-nar-kee) Undivided rule or absolute sovereignty by a single person.

mullah (MOO-LAH) A Muslim teacher or scholar.

obligation (ah-bluh-GAY-shun) Something (as a formal contract or custom) that makes one liable to a course of action.

pilgrimage (PIL-grah-mij) A journey to a shrine or sacred place.

privatization (PRY-vit-iz-AY-shun) To change (as a business) from public to private control or ownership.

qanats (kah-NUTS) Underground water tunnels.

regime (rah-ZHEEM) A type of rule or form of government.

relic (rell-IK) A trace of some past practice, custom, or belief; an object esteemed because of its association with a saint, religious figure, or time period.

sect (SEKT) A group adhering to a distinctive doctrine or to a leader; a religious denomination.

secular (SEH-kyuh-luhr) Not religious.

segregated (SEH-gruh-gayt-ed) To separate or set apart from others or from the general mass.

shah (SHAH) A sovereign of Iran.

FOR MORE INFORMATION

American Islamic Chamber of Commerce
P.O. Box 93033
Albuquerque, NM 87199-3033
Web site: http://www.americanislam.org

Embassy of Islamic Republic of Iran
245 Metcalfe Street
Ottawa, ON K2P 2K2
Canada
(613) 235-4726
e-mail: iranemb@salam.org
Web site: http://www.salamiran.org

ICNA (Islamic Circle of North America)
Book Service
166-26 89th Avenue
Jamaica, NY 11432
(800) 903-0099
e-mail: Books@icna.org

Muslim Students' Association of U.S. and
Canada (MSA-National)
P.O. Box 18612

Washington, DC 20036
(703) 820-7900
e-mail: info@msa-natl.org
Web site: http://www.msa-natl.org

Young Muslims Canada
60 Dundas Street East
P.O. Box 48018
Mississauga, ON L5A 1W0
Canada
Web site: http://www.youngmuslimcanada.org

Web Sites

Due to the changing nature of Internet links, the Rosen Publishing Group, Inc., has developed an online list of Web sites related to the subject of this book. This site is updated regularly. Please use this link to access the list:

http://www.rosenlinks.com/pswc/iran

FOR FURTHER READING

Atefat-Peckham, Susan. *That Kind of Sleep* (National Poetry Series). Minneapolis, MN: Coffee House Press, 2001.

Carboni, Stefano, Alexander Morton, and Marie Swietochowski. *Illustrated Poetry and Epic Images: Persian Painting of the 1330s and 1340s*. New York: Metropolitan Museum of Art, 1994.

Cartlidge, Cherece. *Iran* (Modern Nations). San Diego: Lucent Books, 2002.

Hafiz. *The Gift: Poems by Hafiz the Great Sufi Master*. Translated by Daniel Ladinsky. New York: Penguin, 1999.

Ramen, Fred. *A Historical Atlas of Iran* (Historical Atlases of South Asia, Central Asia, and the Middle East). New York. The Rosen Publishing Group, 2002.

Zeinert, Karen. *The Persian Empire* (Cultures of the Past). Salt Lake City, UT: Benchmark Books, 1997.

BIBLIOGRAPHY

Akrami, Dr. Jamsheed. "Sixty Years of
Film Production in Iran." 1997.
Retrieved June 8, 2002 (http://www.
Encyclopaediairanica.com).

Bagheri, B. "A Wedding, Tehrani Style."
Retrieved June 6, 2002 (http://www.
persianoutpost.com).

CIA World Factbook 2001. "World Factbook—
Iran." 2001. Retrieved June 6, 2002
(http://www.cia.gov/cia/publications/
factbook/index.html).

"Culture and Food." Retrieved June 6, 2002
(http://www.bestirantravel.com).

Fathi, Nazila, "A Little Leg, a Little Booze,
but Hardly Gomorrah." *New York Times*,
April 15, 2002, p. A4.

Fathi, Nazila. "Iranian-American Dancer Is on
Trial in Tehran for 'Corruption.'" *New York
Times*, July 3, 2002, p. A5.

Fathi, Nazila. "Quake in Northern Iran Kills
at Least 500." *New York Times*, June 23,
2002, p. A4.

Fathi, Nazila. "Taboo Surfing: Click Here for
Iran…" *New York Times*, August 4, 2002,
p. C4.

Goodrich, Norma Lorre. *Ancient Myths*. New
York: Meridian Books, 1960.

Kaplan, Gisela, and Rajendra Vijeya. *Cultures
of the World: Iran*. Tarrytown, NY:
Marshall Cavendish Books, 1995.

Klein, Joe. "Shadow Land." *New Yorker*.
February 18 and 25, 2002, pp. 66–76.

MacFarquhar, Neil, "Condom as a Problem
Word: Iran Grapples with a Surge in
Aids." *New York Times*, April 4, 2002,
p. A12

Montaigne, Fen. "Iran: Testing the Waters of
Reform." *National Geographic*, Vol. 196,
No. 1, July 1999, pp. 2–33.

Pearl, Daniel, and Nikhil Deogun. "In Iran,
Coke Bottles Contain Something Else."
Wall Street Journal, July 10, 1998.

Sanders, Renfield. *Places and Peoples of the
World: Iran*. Broomall, PA: Chelsea House
Publishers, 1994.

Taymeeyah, Ibn. "The World of the Jinn."
Translated by Abu Ameenah Bilal Phillips.
Invitation to Islam, January 1998, Issue 4.

West, E. W,. trans. *Sacred Books of the East*,
Vol. 5. Oxford, England: University
Press, 1897.

Yavari, Hamid, and Hossein Mortezaiyan.
"Introduction to Iranian Expatriate Writer,
Mehrnoush Mazarei." *Bonyan* (*Persian
Morning Daily*), March 11, No. 24, 2002,
pp. 5–10.

PRIMARY SOURCE
IMAGE LIST

Page 19: The six swords shown in this photograph are made of bronze and iron and date from 4000 to 650 BC. They are now located at the National Museum of Iran in Tehran, Iran.

Page 20: This wind instrument dates from 4000 to 650 BC and is located at the National Museum of Iran in Tehran.

Page 21: The ruined remains of the tomb of Cyrus the Great, originally discovered in 1951 in Pasargadae, Iran, once the capital of ancient Persia.

Page 22: A present-day aerial photograph of the ruined remains of Persepolis, once the ancient seat of power for kings of the Achaemenid dynasty.

Page 23: This stone relief located at an archaeological site in southern Iran (Naqsh-i Rustam) depicts Ardashir I, also known as Artaxerxes, a king of Persia, and dates from early third century BC.

Page 24: This sixteenth-century Persian miniature depicts Alexander the Great in battle against the Persian army.

Page 26: This fourteenth-century Indian miniature painting of Timur was created between 1336 and 1405.

Page 27: Originally a part of the epic poem *Timurnameh* by Persian poet Abdullah Hatifi, this sixteenth-century painting depicts the capture of Isfahan by Timur's Mongol armies in 1388.

Page 28: The Persian fresco shown on this page depicts Shah Abbas I and is now located at the Chehel Sotun Palace in Isfahan, Iran.

Page 30 (top): This photograph of Reza Khan and his officers was taken January 10, 1925.

Page 30 (bottom): This photograph of a fighter plane was taken at a delivery point of American lend-lease warplanes to Russia.

Page 31: Russian premier Joseph Stalin, U.S. president Franklin Roosevelt, and British prime minister Winston Churchill are pictured in this photograph taken in Tehran, Iran in 1943.

Page 33: A cartoon by Olaf Gulbransson appeared in *Simplicissimus* on July 13, 1908, and depicts Mohammed Ali Shah overthrowing Iran, a nation which outlined its constitution only two years before.

Page 36: This illumination from the *Shahnameh (Book of Kings)* depicts the battle between the Iranians and the Turanians and dates from 1616. It is now housed at the British Library in London, England.

Page 37: The cuneiform writing seen in this contemporary photograph is located within the ruins of Persepolis and dates from 550 to 330 BC.

Page 39: This miniature painting from a manuscript of *One Thousand and One Nights* (also known as the *Arabian Nights*) dates from 1853 to 1859 and is housed at the Golestan Palace Library in Tehran, Iran.

Page 43: The stone relief pictured here is believed to depict King Xerxes and is located in Iran's ancient ruins of Persepolis.

Page 45: This illustration was taken from a fifteenth-century edition of Firdawsi's *Book of Kings* and is housed at the Golestan Palace Library in Tehran, Iran.

Page 46: Zayn Al-Abidin illustrated this painting from Firdawsi's *Book of Kings*. It depicts a bathing scene and dates from 1595. It is now housed at the British Library in London, England.

Page 48: This illustration from an eighteenth-century Scroll of Esther is located in the private collection of Issac Einhorn.

Page 52 and 53: The Iranians pictured in these present-day photographs are celebrating the festival of Sizdeh Bedar, or the last day of the Persian New Year.

Page 55: Iran's supreme leader, Ayatollah Seyed Ali Khamenei, leads a prayer ceremony during the Muslim festival of Eid al-Fitr.

Page 56: Thousands of Iranians are pictured praying at the Imam Khomeini Mosque in Tehran, Iran, during the morning of Eid al-Fitr.

Iran: A Primary Source Cultural Guide

Page 58: The women in this contemporary photograph jump over fire to mark the ancient festival of Shab-e-chahar Shanbeh Suri, literally, the "Eve of Red Wednesday," which is a traditional part of the Iranian New Year festivities.

Page 59: The Muslim woman in this contemporary photograph offers dates to another woman and her child at the Imam Khomeini Mosque during Eid al-Fitr in front of a picture of Iran's late founder of the Islamic Revolution, Ayatollah Ruhollah Khomeini (1902–1989).

Page 60: The Iranian women in this contemporary photograph are in line for a mass wedding ceremony of 1,000 couples.

Page 63: This second-century BC Persian coin is now housed at the Money Museum in Tehran, Iran.

Page 64 (bottom): The brick wall ruins in this contemporary photograph show the ancient city of Susa.

Page 66: This illustration of a Zoroastrian man praying first appeared in the *Illustrated London News* in 1885.

Page 68: This illustration from a Tabriz manuscript dates from 1307 and depicts Muhammad's son-in-law Ali.

Page 69: The Muslims pictured in this contemporary photograph are seen praying during the first day of Ramadan.

Page 71: This Christian illustration, completed between the twelfth and thirteenth centuries, is located at the Armenian Cathedral and Museum in Isfahan, Iran.

Page 73: A contemporary photograph of the ancient ruins of Persepolis.

Page 74: An aerial photograph of present-day Isfahan showing Imam Khomeini Square and the surrounding mosques, most dating from the early seventeenth century.

Page 75 (top): A contemporary photograph depicting Isfahan's Khaju Bridge, originally built in 1650 by Shah Abbas II.

Page 75 (bottom): This ceramic star tile created between the thirteenth and fourteenth century is now located at the Reza Abbasi Museum in Tehran, Iran.

Page 76 (bottom): This Persian miniature painting depicting a royal hunt is dated 1554 and is now located at the National Library of Spain in Madrid, Spain.

Page 77: The Naderi Throne is located at the Golestan Palace in Tehran, Iran.

Page 78 (top): This Indo-Persian carpet dates from the late sixteenth century.

Page 82: This Persian illumination dates from the seventeenth century.

Page 83: A Persian illumination of Mevlâna Jalaluddîn Rumi.

Page 86: This Persian manuscript, an Arabic edition of a Greek book of medicine, *The Materials of Medicine*, is located at the National Library of France in Paris, France.

Page 87: This manuscript illumination depicts music being played during a Persian court of royalty.

Page 88: The manuscript illumination reproduced on this page is by Junaid and dates from 1396. It is now housed at the British Library in London, England.

INDEX

About the Author

Originally from California, Lauren Spencer lives in New York City where she teaches writing workshops in the public schools. In addition to authoring books for young adults, she also writes lifestyle and music articles for magazines.

Designer: Geri Fletcher; **Cover Designer:** Tahara Hasan; **Editor:** Jill Jarnow; **Photo Researcher:** Gillian Harper; **Photo Research Assistant:** Fernanda Rocha